MW00795535

A Shot in the Dark

A Daily Dose of Inspiration for Your Soul

Printed in the United States of America

First Printing, 2019

ISBN 978-0-9994726-2-0

Happie Face Publishing Company
www.hfpublishingco.com

A Word from Mark Corbin, the author:

The funny thing about life is that you have to live it in order to get through it. There have been days that were too tough to even get out of bed, but I was taught that no matter how bad you feel, if you can go, then get up and go. It is only by the grace of God that any of us make it through the course of a day, week, month, or year and surely, we never make the journey alone. I have been blessed and encouraged by my friends to create A Shot in the Dark and in these pages you will read of the struggles, disappointment, pain, joy, and love we all need to get through each day. If by chance you pick up this devotional, my prayer is that you find wisdom, laughter, and the word of God to encourage you to keep on living through life.

If you enjoy *A Shot in the Dark*, feel free to listen to the daily podcast at anchor.fm/mark-corbin. Thank you.

Mark Corbin

Bible verses are from the New King James Version (NKJV)
& the King James Version (KJV)

Day 1: Not Every Fight Will Be a Gun Fight

There are three rules to fighting:

Rule 1: Get Home
Rule 2: Fights Don't Have Rules
Rule 3: Refer to Rule #1

Prepare your body and mind for all possible scenarios. In gun fights, you have to perfect your aim, in fist fights, you hit to win, and in a screaming match, you leave dogs barking at the moon.

Your life belongs to those you love. Make sure you share it with them.

Scripture of the day: Psalm 144:1
"Blessed be the Lord my strength which teacheth my hands to war, and my fingers to fight."

Day 2: Put 'em Up
"I'm a fighter." – Unknown

This one leaves us with a few good points. *I am a fighter –* make that decision now. It does not matter who others think who you are.

I will not give up – the hardest thing in the world to do is to keep going when everything around you calls for your surrender.

I will stumble and fall but I will stand back up – in the midst of my errors, I will show and do my best. I am not allowed to *ever* quit.

It might take me longer than most but I will stand up and fight – yes, it is hard, but get up.

I will always get up.

Scripture of the day: 2 Corinthians 10:3-5
"For though we walk in the flesh, we do not war according to the flesh. For the weapons of our warfare are not carnal but mighty in God for pulling down strongholds, casting down arguments and every high thing that exalts itself against the knowledge of God, bringing every thought into captivity to the obedience of Christ,"

Day 3: Dogs Don't Chase at Parked Cars

"It's better to cross the line and suffer the consequences than to just stare at that line for the rest of your life." – Unknown

I have that quote hanging on my wall to serve as a push for me to do something this year that I have been putting off. I have made plans in the past, written them down, and put the plan into action only to stop repeatedly because of: a personal or professional obstacle, someone close to me disapproved, or because of fear. Finally, I would find myself reading my list of plans only to be disappointed by what I had not done and not happy for what I had accomplished.

I spoke with my dad about how and why we find ourselves on the move chasing things that we do not really want and then attaining the very thing that does not make us happy.

He simply said, "Son, do you remember the dog that lived on the street in front of your grandmother's house? Yes, the dog that would chase the cars up and down the street as they drove by? Yes, that dog." He went on to tell me that *dogs do not chase after parked cars.*

"So son, continue to move on the path that God has given you."

Scripture of the day: Isaiah 64:8
"But now, O LORD, You are our Father; we are the clay, and You our potter; and all we are the work of Your hand."

Day 4: Know Your Powers

"Know your powers. The power of your words, your silence, your mind, your body language and your body itself. Control them." – Sonya Teclai

Read and listen to yourself with care:
1. Your words – always know that no matter where you are, someone is listening to you. Speak kindly and choose your words carefully.
2. Your silence – sometimes it's best not say anything at all, but there are moments when you should speak only to improve the silence.
3. Your mind – no one likes a know-it-all, but if what you know can help God's people, then share the knowledge.
4. Your body language and body – unfold your arms and uncross your legs. Stop being defensive and be open and free.

Two warriors were surrounded, and they had to fight their way out. As they fought and annihilated their attackers, one warrior noticed that his counterpart hit one of the attackers and the attacker looked as if he had been broken into two pieces. The warrior turned to the other and asked, "how hard did you hit him?" The other warrior smiled and said, "I hit him as hard as I could."

So today my friend, know your power and when you encounter an attacker, smile and hit them as hard as you can.

Scripture of the day: Deuteronomy 3:22
"Ye shall not fear them: for the Lord your God shall fight for you."

Day 5: Decide

"So do it. Decide. Is this your life the life you want to live? Is this the person you want to love? Is this the best you can be? Can you be stronger? Kinder? More compassionate? Decide. Breathe in. Breathe out and decide." – from *Grey's Anatomy*

"Decide" is a call to action. It forces us to deal with our worry, procrastination, doubt, and fear. When I played football, we had a saying – "if you scared, say you sacred." Then we would go do the thing, so I'm telling you – go do the thing.

Is this the life you want to live? There can only be two answers – yes or no. If the answer is no, change your life. If the answer is yes, then share your joy.

Is this the person you want to love? It feels good loving somebody when somebody loves you back. If they don't love you back, take action and decide.

Is this the best you can be? You worked hard to get here, but what could you change to be an even better you? Don't do it for him or her, and most definitely don't do it for them. This change is about *you* and your magnificent self.

Can you be stronger? You can *always* be stronger mentally, spiritually, and physically. Buy a book and build your mind, pray daily and go to church, and do some push-ups and you'd be surprised what a few of those will do to your body.

Can you be kinder? Smile at people. Smile a *real* smile and say hello. You will also be surprised how that smile will impact someone's day.

Decide. You can do it. The time has come for you to take action. Breathe in and breathe out. The only way to get this wrong today is to do nothing.

Decide.

Scripture of the day: Matthew 18:18-19
"Verily I say unto you, Whatsoever ye shall bind on earth shall be bound in heaven: and whatsoever ye shall loose on earth shall be loosed in heaven. Again, I say unto you, that if two of you shall agree on earth as touching any thing that they shall ask, it shall be done for them of my Father which is in heaven."

Day 6: When Fear Knocks...

"When fear knocks, let faith answer the door." – Robin
Roberts

Nothing will be there. First of all, fear *is* real. Fear is a
feeling that grips us all at some points in our lives; we are
afraid of our ideas being met with disappointment, afraid of
starting a business, afraid of stepping out of our comfort
zone, afraid of falling.

I am convinced that fear is only what we allow it to be. We
all know that unfortunately the "big bad" is going to come
knocking at our door. The problem is we spend too much
time waiting on a knock that may never come.

First, prepare yourself for all fights, whether, physical,
mental, or spiritual and prepare to win. Now, be clear – there
are real things out there that will get you. But if you prepare
for the fight mentally and physically, you *will* win. So, the
next time fear rings your bell or knocks, you can knock back.

Scripture of the day: Isaiah 41:10
*"Fear thou not; for I am with thee: be not dismayed; for I
am thy God: I will strengthen thee; yea, I will help thee; yea,
I will uphold thee with the right hand of my righteousness."*

Day 7: I Got One Rock

"The difference between who you are and who you want to be is what you do." – Bill Phillips

We all have hard times and sometimes those hard times have us and we seem to not be able to overcome anything at all. The Charlie Daniels Band has a song called "The Devil Went Down to Georgia" (good song by the way) and one of the lines is: *"The devil went down to Georgia for a soul to steal. He was in a bind because he was way behind and he was willing to make a deal."*

First thing's first – the devil doesn't deal.

So, in good and tough times, we must always be willing to fight hand to hand, stick to stick, and brick to brick. When the devil comes looking for me and you, we must do as David did – go down to the water and not get us smooth stones but go and get our rock. You only need one.

Imagine picking up a rock. Look at it – one side says God, one side says Jesus, and around the middle it reads Holy Spirit. Reach into your back pocket and take out your sling. Put your rock in your sling and now start swinging.

Today, when the enemy shows up, throw your rock and slay your enemy.

Scripture of the day: Psalm 18:2
"The Lord is my rock, and my fortress, and my deliverer, my God, my strength in whom I will trust; my buckler, and the horn of my salvation, and my high tower."

Day 8: Lions, Tigers, and Bears – Okay. I'm a Wolf

"The tiger, the bear, and the lion may be more powerful, but the wolf doesn't perform in a circus." – Unknown

Being a wolf is about being different, embracing your differentness and celebrating who you are.

All four animals are similar – they are pack animals, have a dominance hierarchy, and the dominant male leads the group. I chose the wolf today because I know you are trying new things this year and because your new-found courage will be met with some resistance. There will be those you know who will want you to get back in your circus cage and perform like the other caged lions, tigers, and bears but you must resist. You will hear them say, "Oh, you want to be a lone wolf? That's not good."

When you hear that noise, don't you flinch. Don't you dare go back to that circus. Embrace your inner wolf and remember this: wolves come in packs of six to ten – find your wolf pack. Wolves possess high intelligence and strong instincts and loyalty – it will not be caged to balance on some ball, jump through some hoop, or let somebody put their head in its mouth.

That is not you, so be you – be a wolf.

Scripture of the day: Luke 10:19
"Behold, I give unto you power to tread on serpents and scorpions, and over all the power of the enemy, and nothing shall by any means hurt you."

Day 9: Speak Power, Love, Truth, Strength, and Courage to Your Inner Warrior

"Do not speak badly of yourself, for the warrior within hears your words and is lessened by them." – David Gemmell

We all make the mistake of either saying or doing something we think is stupid, crazy, insane, and dumb, but we must permanently remove those negative words from our vocabulary. You and I as warriors fighting daily battles must not allow negativity to gain a foothold in our minds. Negative self-talk attacks our warrior in four ways:
1. When the negative thought appears in your mind's eye.
2. When you speak the negative thought aloud.
3. You hear the negative word spoken.
4. The negative thought now marinates in your spirit.

It's tough enough to go into battle each day with enemies who want to devour and kill you, let alone to overcome ourselves in order to win a fight you are already in. So, from this day forward, we must speak power, truth, and strength to our warrior selves.

Affirmation for today: I will defeat every enemy. There is no mountain that can stand in my way. I will hit hard those that seek my demise. I will love completely those who love me. Let there be no doubt that I will defend my family and those that I love with my last breath. I will lay my burdens down.

Scripture of the day: Mark 11:23
"For verily I say unto you, That whosoever shall say unto this mountain, Be thou removed, and be thou cast into the sea; and shall not doubt in his heart, but shall believe that those things which he saith shall come to pass; he shall have whatsoever he saith."

14

Day 10: Believe in Yourself

In high school before each football game, my football coach would play the song, "Believe" sung by Lena Horne from The Wiz. He would have us all in the locker room or gym, depending on where we played, with the lights off as the song played. I would lay there on the floor with my helmet on and with my eyes closed and could visualize the words of the song as it played. That's how I remember my favorite lines:

> *"Believe in yourself right from the start... believe in the magic inside of your heart... believe all these things not because I told you to... but believe in yourself as I believe in you."*

That that song was the difference between me staying in Washington, D.C. and earning a scholarship to Central State University. So, I say to you today, believe in yourself. You must believe that all your desires can be yours. No one else can make your dreams come true – take it from a knock-kneed little boy, who was never supposed to play football. Your belief in yourself is about you.

Your belief in you must be displayed in your walk. Your belief in you must be displayed your talk – speak confidently and hold your head up, and your belief in you must be displayed in your presence – own every room you walk in and fill the room with your smile. You must believe in you no matter what! There will be days that no matter what you do, yours will be the only smile you will see.

I urge you to believe in yourself no matter the obstacle, person, or demon from hell that appears – don't you doubt you!

Believe! Believe in yourself from the start and believe in the magic in your heart.

Scripture of the day: Luke 8:50
"But when Jesus heard it, he answered him, saying, Fear not: believe only, and she shall be made whole."

Day 11: It's You.

"It's not who you are that holds you back, it's who you think you're not." – Denis Waitley

Have you ever noticed how in the midst of you working hard to achieve, you forget who you are? You look up one day and you do not recognize yourself? I mean, you know it's you, but it's not the you that you thought you would be; a bad decision here and there, a circumstance beyond your control and bam! You have become complicit in a version of your life you would not have imagined when you were growing up.

Do you remember the you that you dreamt of becoming when you were a child? I want you to close your eyes and picture yourself as a kid. Now remember what you dreamt of becoming? A teacher? A politician, a superstar, a lawyer, a fireman, or maybe a chef? Now open your eyes and think of what you should do next. First, remember that optimistic feeling, then remember why you had the dream in the first place, and lastly, say to yourself, I can do it.

You are all the help you need. Trust your faith and believe you can do it.

Scripture of the day: Joshua 1:9
"Have not I commanded thee? Be strong and of a good courage; be not afraid, neither be thou dismayed: for the Lord thy God is with thee whithersoever thou goest."

Day 12: Remember, It's a New Day – Own It!

"If you know me based on who I was a year ago, you don't know me at all. My growth game is strong. Allow me to reintroduce myself." – Aagam Shah

You are not the same person you were a year ago. Those who cast you in the movie of your life that plays on the screens of their minds have no idea who you are. Do not be dismayed when they cast you as timid, afraid, scared, or useless. We cannot buy into the labels others give us. Cast yourself as the hero in your own life.

Yes, my friend – you are the hero; small children love you, grandmothers adore you, and men and women want to be you – even those who pretend not to know your name. It is a new day and your growth game is strong. You built your strength wiping away the tears no one saw you cry. No one saw you walk through hell and watch the devil hold the door open because he was glad you got out.

Now, you are ready. You got a smile that lights up rooms, and people want to know who you are, so you tell them you are mighty, strong, blessed, loved, prepared, rough and tough and ready to rumble.

Scripture of the day: Isaiah 41:13
"For I the Lord thy God will hold thy right hand, saying unto thee, Fear not; I will help thee."

Day 13: The Number One Reason

"The number one reason why people give up so fast is because they tend to look at how far they still have to go instead of how far they have gotten." – Unknown

It's funny when you think about it, but we give up on ourselves much faster than we would give up on a friend or a bad habit and sometimes the line is so blurry that we can't tell the bad habit from the friend. When you look at it, it's a valuable lesson; we are taught to value important things like time, money, and people. Amazing, isn't it? All the things on the list are necessary and important and it is the list worthy of sharing. However, it's a new day and we must now add a new and equally important component to the list – yourself.

You must add yourself because by direct extension, your goals are inclusive of others, but we lose sight of ourselves. What I mean is, we will cease pursing our goals if there is a cry in the dark from our job, family, or friends. The cry in the dark is real or imagined and is meant to move you into a different state of being away from your priorities and to those of your group a path that is not consistent with your chosen path.

To me, *self* is inclusive of those whom you care about and *yourself* is only exclusive to you. Yes, value self; it is good to do so, however, please begin to value yourself because one day you will be gone, and you will blame yourself for being alone and a stranger to yourself.

I believe giving up on yourself is an extension of how we process visual ques as opposed to a negative verbal interaction. Think of it this way: the house I once lived in is on a hill. I would go out from time to time and run on that hill. Surely, running up and down the hill was a physical challenge, but what made running up the hill difficult was at the top of the hill, there was a STOP sign. Processing that constant negative visual queue while moving forward is a part of the duality that men and women face daily as they move towards accomplishing their goals.

Scripture of the day: Colossians 1:11-12
"Strengthened with all might, according to his glorious power, unto all patience and longsuffering with joyfulness; Giving thanks unto the Father, which hath made us meet to be partakers of the inheritance of the saints in light."

Day 14: It Does Not Matter

"No matter what happens, no matter how far you seem to be away from where you want to be, never stop believing that you will somehow make it. Have an unrelenting belief that things will work out, that the long road has a purpose, that the things that you desire may not happen today, but they will happen. Continue to persist and persevere." – Brad Gast.

Alright – all the I's have been dotted and all the T's have been crossed. Clothes are clean, bag is all packed, car was gassed up the night before and now, the car won't start. As you stand behind the line of "pisstivity" and full-blown rage, take a deep breath, move away from the line, call a cab, and go slay your presentation!

You see, it does not matter what happens. You are still closer to your greatness today than yesterday. You are strong and smart and as long as you continue believing in yourself, you could find you way out of a dark cave blindfolded. You have gotten to this point in your life by never giving up on you. This is not luck or timing – you have prepared yourself.

Every fight and argument won and lost against your enemies have strengthened you. Even before you put one foot on your path, the stop signs were there. You looked down that long road and grabbed your bag full of purpose and took the first step, then another, and then another. Nothing can top you or stop you. You now bring a mature mind to your purpose. You can have it all but now we know we will take our successes one at a time.

Do not stop. Do not give up. Do not quit. Persist and persevere and you can have all you dream of.

Scripture of the day: Romans 12:12
"Rejoicing in hope, patient in tribulation, continuing instant in prayer."

Day 15: Kick the Door Open!

"It's amazing how drastically your life can change when you stop accepting things you hate." – Steve Maraboli

In this season of change, we must make the change we have decided. We *say* we want to change, but we tend not to put the change we want into effect.

The word drastic means "likely to have a strong or far reaching effect; radical or extreme." So, yes, it's time to embrace that new direction and walk away from things you hate. Stop going back because you know it isn't going to change or get better. It's like being in your car on a single lane street and there is a car blocking your path forward and back. You want to back up, so you look into the mirror and see the warning that you've seen a million times – *objects in the mirror appear closer than they actually are.*

I think the urge to stop and/or go back is about being comfortable. We go back to feeling bad and being treated bad because it has become our norm. Here's the great thing about a new day – it's the perfect chance to begin a new normal. As Maria Kumar put it, "become your own responsibility."

You are incredible!

This life still has a lot of living left in it. Kick the door open on your possibilities and don't look back. Go get your greatness.

Scripture of the day: Philippians 4:13
"I can do all things through Christ which strengthens me."

Day 16: Her Soul

"Her soul was too deep to swim in for those who only want to swim in the shallow end." – A.J. Lawless

The great things about deep, soulful women is that the last thing you see is their soul. Surely you take in her beauty when she walks in a room and when she walks by, you get caught up in her essence trailing behind her and you linger like a little boy staring at a jet stream in the sky. However, her beauty and essence are only for those who cannot handle the depth of her soul. Her power is quiet and sits alone, not wanting to be disturbed, but if you are so foolish as to bother those she loves and what she holds sacred, you will not know you have been cut until you get home.

The depth of her soul is where weak men, old lovers, and fools have gone to skip rocks, as their game was not tight and their minds not right enough to understand where to stand in her life. There are only three places for you to stand: you can stand beside her building a love, stand in front of her to fight all the obstacles those who would attack her, or stand behind her and celebrate the woman she is. The weak see you and mock you because of how you stand, but that's the problem with what they don't understand. When you move into the depths of her soul, you will finally understand how great a gift God has sent, because you have found the rib that fits.

Scripture of the day: Luke 1:45
"And blessed is she that believed: for there shall be a performance of those things which were told her from the Lord."

Day 17: Rest

After drawing lines in the sand, slaying dragons, and defeating the thief who came to kill, steal, and destroy your dreams and your life, you managed to pull a rabbit out of your hat – all within 60 hours through rough, cold, and snowy days. Now it's time to take the cape off.

Take your mind off the grind. Draw a circle around yourself and free your mind. No stress, no strife. Spend some time being happy today.

Rest.

Scripture of the day: Matthew 11:28-30
"Come unto me, all ye that labour and are heavy laden, and I will give you rest. Take my yoke upon you, and learn of me; for I am meek and lowly in heart: and ye shall find rest unto your souls. For my yoke is easy, and my burden is light."

Day 18: Run the Play That Is Called

"When the devil keeps asking you to look at your past, there must be something good in the future he doesn't want you to see." – Unknown

You have worked on your game strategy and you've decided that you will start the day with a win. You've made your bed, you said your devotion, and reviewed your goals (*how much money do you want to make, how many people you are going to help, etc.*). Stand there and call the play in the huddle. You get to the threshold and just before you walk out the door, the enemy shows up like an opposing defense and reminds you of who you used to be, but you are ready to run the play called in your huddle.

You know your assignment – keep your head on a swivel and go hard on every play. Achieve your goals by building a financial fence around your family, being honorable, respecting your loved ones, and speaking truth to power. The enemy is going to try to show you your past, but we will not take an emotional loss this week. Take one more look in the mirror before you take the field of life today.

This is what you tell yourself: Average guys want to be good, good guys want to be great, and great guys want to be you. The only thing getting tuned out today are the lies, hatred, and doubt. Go out there and do our best.

Scripture of the day: John 10:10
"The thief cometh not, but for to steal, and to kill, and to destroy: I am come that they might have life, and that they might have it more abundantly."

Day 19: Be Strong; You Are Built to Win

"You are far too smart to be the only thing standing in your way." – Jennifer Freeman

Today, we will not procrastinate or let doubt in. There is no room for tiredness. There are so many things that could possibly get in the way today – apathy, fatigue, anger, lust, envy, neglect, people, and fear – but don't let any of these things stand in your way and more importantly, don't become your own obstacle.

Today, we will run over anyone and anything that gets in our way. Today you will stand tall and you will be the reason your enemies fail.

Say this to yourself: *During this growing season, I am watered by the sweet sounds of positivity. During this growing season, I will till and cultivate the soil of my mind and body, lifting heavy and consuming new knowledge. I will stand in the light of the sun having been redeemed. I am made stronger and I am now fit for this fight. I am built from head to toe, strong, mighty, swift, and fast. I stand tall and no longer afraid of what might happen.*

Now for one final check before you go to battle: your mind is made up? Check. Your arms are strong? Check. Your feet pointed in the right direction? Check. Your vision is clear? Check. Shoulders are broad and mighty? Check. Legs are fit and firm? Check.

Yes, you are built for only one thing – to win.

Scripture of the day: Ephesians 6:11
"Put on the whole armour of God, that ye may be able to stand against the wiles of the devil."

Day 20: Master Your Day

"You are a fighter. Look at everything you've overcome. Don't give up now." – Olivia Benson from *Law & Order: SVU*

So let's go over the facts:
1. You are a fighter – no matter what people think, you like a good fight. You won't pick a fight, but you will end one.
2. Look at everything you've overcome; being hungry, being tired, and you have overcome the objections of petty people.
3. Don't give up now. You can't stop and you won't stop. You can dig deeper and when people mess with you, they will find that they will be met with only two options – pain or pleasure – and the choice will be theirs to decide.

Be clear about who and what you have become; you are a fighter, so rise and slay your giants every day.

Scripture of the day: Deuteronomy 7:21
"Thou shalt not be affrighted at them: for the Lord thy God is among you, a mighty God and terrible."

Day 21: I Am the Fire

"The best thing you could do is master the chaos in you. You are not thrown into the fire, you *are* the fire." – Mama Indigo

Chaos is "complete disorder and confusion", but let's get something straight. – just because people don't understand your methods and process does not mean that there is disorder and confusion within you. The thing about the problems people have when they look at you is that what's reflected at them is not your reflection. What they see is what they lack, don't have, or don't know how to get. The fact of the matter is, sure, you were living a chaotic existence while trying to please, explain, and make people dig you, but you finally realized that all these supposed fires that you've battled day in and day out were not meant to consume you.

Say this out loud: *I am fire! All this time, you've been trying to put fires out asking why all the pressure and why are all the train wrecks happening at my station? It's because you are fire.* Being the fire requires you to do something different, so here's your fire list: walk out with your head held high and be confident because if you are the fire, you've got to hold your torch high today. Pause for a minute and feel that heat rising within you. Now, people who pretend to ignore you can't do it today. Your light will shine so bright that some people will have to just look away and let's not forget to mention that the heat from your fire is going to feel so good that they will just want to be close to you. All you have to do now is use your fire responsibly; some will be consumed by it and you don't want to get burned by it either.

Scripture of the day: Proverbs 27:17
"Iron sharpeneth iron; so a man sharpeneth the countenance of his friend."

Day 22: You Are A Winner

Some of what you may hear is cliché, but it's true. You embraced who you are this week, you did not allow others to hold you back, you met every challenge, you stepped out on faith despite it being difficult, and for the first time in a long time, you feel good about you. You notice your thinking and focus has changed. What I mean is, up until this point, you had been concerned with getting the victory. I think getting the victory is great, but we want the victory at the expense of winning.

Surely, most of us see ourselves standing on the podium, hands held high celebrating the victory at the end of our race, but most neglect the daily struggle – it's the little wins that make the victory sweet. Think about it – no one knows of your daily struggle of just getting out bed.

That's a win.

No one knows of the tears you "cry from your soul" about relevance, being smart enough, tough enough or pretty enough, but you get up and go every day.

That's a win.

You love so hard sometimes that even you wonder why you put up with him.

That's a win.

You are so brave – yes, brave because living life with patience and kindness, seeking knowledge and truth, and displaying your vulnerability and still managing to pull it together to get to Friday without hurting anybody or yourself.

That's a win.

That, my friend, is a win! If you think about it, the sheer fact that you locked your crazy in the closet this week is a win.

Take some time today and count your wins because there is at least one. Be fair in your assessment of yourself; stop being so critical and measuring yourself using someone else's ruler.

Scripture of the day: 1 Corinthians 9:24
"Know ye not that they which run in a race run all, but one receiveth the prize? So run, that ye may obtain."

Day 23: It's the Freakin' Weekend

All week long, you ran from one fire to another and put each and every one of them out. You got so good at putting out fires, people started calling you Smokey the Bear. You made multitasking look so easy that people thought you had four hands, two brains, and a robot. Bad news bounced off you so often even you had to check to see if you had on a bullet proof vest. You have finally embraced the concept that if it was not for the last minute, some people could not get anything done.

You realized that people don't call you for the easy or fun projects – not even for the stuff where you need to pull a rabbit out of a hat. No, they call you when they need to make a dollar out of 15 cents and that's after they have already taken away the dime.

Here's the best part – you made it! As you enjoy your time off, you can smile and say quietly, *"Got 'em."*

Scripture of the day: Galatians 6:9
"And let us not be weary in well doing: for in due season we shall reap, if we faint not."

Day 24: The Clock is Ticking

"Tomorrow is too late, yesterday is over and now is exactly the right moment, so start." – Unknown

The clock is ticking. You only have 24 hours to do what needs to be done today.

Tomorrow is too late – no need to put that person or thing off. Whatever needs to be done will not be easier tomorrow and whatever needs to be said will not sound better tomorrow.

Yesterday is over – the funny thing about yesterday is that only after it has passed do you realize how strong you really are. Now, the clock is ticking, and I have three questions for you: Did you make the plan? Did you write the plan? Are you ready to work the plan? Tick, tock, the clock is ticking.

Now is exactly the right moment to start – you are exactly where you are supposed to be. I know you thought you would be doing something else, be somewhere else, and with someone else, but *here* is where you are and *here* is where you should be. This is your time, and this is exactly the right moment to be you.

Tomorrow isn't here yet, and yesterday is gone. You must decide to start right now! Decide to start living, loving, and being great!

Scripture of the day: Isaiah 43:19
"Behold, I will do a new thing; now it shall spring forth; shall ye not know it? I will even make a way in the wilderness, and rivers in the desert."

Day 25: It Ain't That Far

"Don't be afraid of the space between your dreams and reality. If you can dream it, you can make it so." - Belva Davis

Stop being afraid of who you are and stop with the false starts. You know what to do. If you don't know, I will help you find a way.

By now you know the only person that is holding you back is you and frankly, you are too strong and smart to be the reason you fail. There's one thing for certain and two things for sure – you are strong and smart and can have whatever you set your mind to.

The distance between having and not having isn't that far. You can make your dreams come true, but first you must call that thing out.

I dare you to do it – to become the man or woman you wanted to be when you were a child. There is still time.

Scripture of the day: Matthew 21:22
"And all things, whatsoever ye shall ask in prayer, believing, ye shall receive."

Day 26: She's Built for This

"Don't look for a princess in need of saving. Search for a queen willing to fight by your side." – Unknown

The drums of war are beating off in the distance. Unknown enemies threaten to topple your kingdom and you look to your left and your right and find that you are alone. Your squad is tight – they fight in the distance holding legions at bay. You continue to fight through and over every obstacle that gets in your way just to get to her. Cutting through fences, smashing barricades and even banging your head against some walls.

You fight your way through with shield and buckler and sword at the ready. She is not in need of saving. She can and will fight alone. She is well equipped to do what needs to be done. She has told you before, "Babe, I'm built for this." This is the fight to vanquish all enemies. Not everyone is willing to build a kingdom to launch an empire. In this battle a "boo" will not do. A "ride or die" is fine, but that implies that there are options. This fight requires a grown woman. A grown woman vanquishes doubt and her words are different. A grown woman understands you got a little dirt on you, and truth be told, she ain't squeaky clean either.

Finally, a grown woman is here, standing at your right side sword and shield at the ready. You both lookout towards the horizon, not at what's coming. Today, you both move towards the horizon to get what you have claimed.

Scripture of the day: Luke 1:45
"And blessed is she that believed: for there shall be a performance of those things which were told her from the Lord."

Day 27: This Is a Test

"If it's meant for you, you won't have to beg for it. You will never have to sacrifice your dignity for your destiny." – Edgar Allen Poe

Dignity: The state or quality of being worthy of honor or respect.

Destiny: The events that will necessarily happen to a particular person or thing in the future.

Before you respond to supercilious comments this morning, quietly go to that closet you have your crazy locked in and firmly place your hand on the door and say: *this is a test and for the next eight hours, I will be who I am: strong and mighty, bold and loved, confident and humble.* Understand that this test today is to find out if what you believe is true. Are you sure you want what you claimed? Do you really believe your prayers will be answered?

Monday, they thought they scared you. Tuesday, they thought the isolation would bother you. Wednesday, you're still trying to figure out what that giant waste of time they called a meeting was about. Yes, this is a test, but be very clear, it isn't your test. Your enemies do not understand what happened to you. They cannot recognize that your change is not a new year's resolution or some new diet and that's okay – let your enemies do what enemies do.

Look, you will never have to sacrifice yourself, your honor or your self-respect for what's already yours.

Be bold, be diligent, and be you. Go get what's already yours!

Scripture of the day: James 1:2-3
"My brethren, count it all joy when you fall into various trials, knowing that the testing of your faith produces patience."

Day 28: Exclamation Point Day

You have two choices, and this isn't up for debate: Go or don't go – and don't go isn't a choice. Of course you are tired and you don't like those people, but you have to go. Frankly, if you were going to quit, you should have quit with the rest of them.

The fact of the matter is we don't quit, so get it out of your mind. We got work to do.

So let's go through our checklist:
- Your heart is beating? Check.
- You are breathing? Check.
- You have 10 fingers and 10 toes? Check.
- You aren't dead? Check.

It's time to go.

It doesn't matter what they think when you show up because a weaker man or woman would have stayed home. Not you – you came to put in work.

It's exclamation point day, but you have to make a choice; how will this week end? With a comma, period, or an exclamation point? Go do what needs to be done.

Scripture of the day: 2 Corinthians 8:11
"But now you also must complete the doing of it; that as there was a readiness to desire it, so there also may be a completion out of what you have."

Day 29: You Made It

You made it! You deserve to be on the corner of Awesome and Bomb Diggity today. I don't know about you, but I am so happy with my results, I am sweating chocolate milk. Let's follow Eleanor Brown's advice:

"Self-care is so important. When you take time to replenish your spirit, it allows you to serve others from the overflow. You cannot serve from an empty vessel."

Get filled up and replenished by doing what you do.

Scripture of the day: 1 Corinthians 10:31
"Therefore, whether you eat or drink, or whatever you do, do all to the glory of God."

Day 30: Here We Go!

Here are the numbers to know:

- There are approximately 125 million men and women employed in the United States.
- You will work approximately eight hours a day.
- There will be only one critical hour of those eight hours – you decide that hour.
- Of that 125 million, there is only one person that matters – and you are that one.

Now let us take a step to make progress.

Put your arms out wide and look from fingertip to fingertip. No one's reach shall be greater than your reach today. Keep your arms out wide and make a muscle – there will be nobody stronger than you today. Look at your shoulders – there are no shoulders broader and more capable of bearing a heavier load than yours today.

Now let us finish strong.

Mirror, mirror on the wall, I am the baddest of them all! This year is my year to have all that I claim. I will raise bars and knock down walls.

Scripture of the day: Proverbs 3:5-6
"Trust in the Lord with all your heart, and lean not on your own understanding; In all your ways acknowledge Him, and He shall direct your paths."

Day 31: Cause of Growth

"A man grows with the greatness of his task." – Joseph Lynch from the movie, *Assassin's Creed*

Reading and hearing those words got me to thinking about age and maturity, which are not the same. Each day, no matter how well you plan, your task brings with it a certain amount of intrigue, truth, and excitement. Today will bring more of the same. Your greatness will not be determined by the completion of tasks. It will be determined by the level of determination, grace and mercy, and humility you utilize in completing your task.

Do not allow your approach to routine task to be light and trite because a job well done does not require it being done again. Grace and mercy must be used in abundance because once your foe has been defeated and your victory is secure, your foe must be left with their dignity. The burden of humility grows with every job well done. Humility is a weight that only seems heavy when you carry the weight of success alone. Lighten your load – help someone else become great.

You have felt greatness calling you for some time now and you have refused to answer the call. Now look what's happened – instead of running out to meet your greatness, it has tracked you down. When the moment for you to be great arrives, here's what you should do: look into your palm and say quietly to yourself, *I am great and wonderfully made.*

Scripture of the day: Proverbs 16:3
"Commit your works unto the Lord, and your thoughts will be established."

Day 32: Choose a Flavor

"She is both hellfire and holy water and the flavor you taste depends on how you treat her." – Sneha Pal

Before your eyes can see, the light of the world is tinted by your mother's love. The first sound we hear is the beating heart of a woman and for the vast majority of us, the first time we are exposed to something new is because a woman cared enough to share.

The great duality of women is only made deeper by their complicity and dominance. Complicity because they choose to love, they suffer through the growth of that love, even when that love drags complacency, disrespect, and even neglect along with it. A dominance so magnificent that we tend not to notice until it is brandished like a fiery sword when she has been pushed too far.

Yet, a woman's power calms our fears, heals our wounds and encourages one to exceed their grasp.

So take your seat at her table and be prepared to be served. She will only be serving two drinks – hell fire or holy water. You can have your fill of one or the other, but remember the flavor you taste depends on how you treat her.

Choose wisely.

Scripture of the day: Proverbs 31:30
"Charm is deceitful and beauty is passing, but a woman who fears the Lord, she shall be praised."

Day 33: The Bar Has Been Raised

"You don't have to be better than everybody else. You just have to be better than you used to be." – Wayne W. Dyer

You are slowly beginning to realize this isn't an ordinary year for you. Although you are the same person, everything about you has begun to change. You've pushed away from the shore and you are now moving out into the deep water, but when you look around, no one is there. Surely your squad is on deck, praying, cheering, and willing to smash all haters.

But out here in the deep water is where change is going to come. Out here, everybody else is a metaphor for me, myself, and I. Out here, right now; you have to be better than you have ever been. You must be more courageous, stronger, smarter, faster, smoother, and intentional about your future.

Today will not be tomorrow; what you do today, who you choose to love, be kind to, and who you have to smack today. You've changed and *everyone* around you knows it. Stay the course you have created despite the winds blowing or the waves tossing. When you make it out of the deep water, you will be better than you have ever been.

Stay the course.

Scripture of the day: Psalm 143:10
"Teach me to do your will, for you are my God. Your spirit is good. Lead me in the land of uprightness."

Day 34: Forward into Growth

"In any given moment, we have two options: to step forward into growth or to step back into safety." – Abraham Maslow

The greatest challenge of being alive is living. We are all alive but we are not living and most of us are not living the life of our dreams. At the turn of the century, the mining industry would put canaries in a cage and lower the cage into a mine. If the canary was alive when they pulled the cage back, then it was safe to go into the mine.

You and I have been the canary for far too long, trapped in someone else's mine, that we don't know fresh air from a foul odor. The time has come to make a choice to get fresh air or remain in the foul odor.

Now, here's a warning: once your life knows you are starting to live, it will try to pull, drag, and trap you back into that "mish-mash of mediocrity" you called a life. You will hear, *I miss the old you, I'm going to need you to...* or *I like the way you used to...* but it's time to step forward. It's time to create your own lane and move out into the deep water. All the magnificent gifts of living are in the deep water, so you must choose to either step forward into growth or back into mediocrity.

Scripture of the day: Isaiah 41:10
"Fear not, for I am with you; be not dismayed, for I am your God. I will strengthen you, yes, I will help you, I will uphold you with My righteous right hand."

Day 35: You Are Amazing

You are amazing! No really – let me tell you about yourself:

1. You stepped forward into living.
2. You have started to create your own lane for your success.
3. You have raised the bar and you are a changed soul.
4. You gobbled up goals and displayed skills this week that blew the average mind.
5. You stepped out into the deep water.
6. You stopped allowing silly spectator voices to hold you back.
7. You have embraced the duality of your complicity to love and be loved.
8. You've taken firm hold of your power and strength to mold, calm, and shape those around you.
9. Your determination is bottomless because you have decided that nothing can stop you.
10. Your grace and mercy have replaced anger.
11. You've learned to smile and laugh out loud.
12. You believe you are smart.
13. You believe you are strong.
14. You believe you are courageous.
15. You have strength and power you have not used yet!

I am proud of you.

You will be even better next week.

Scripture of the day: Colossians 1:10
"That you may walk worthy of the Lord, fully pleasing Him, being fruitful in every good work and increasing in the knowledge of God."

Day 36: Mountain-Moving Day

"You have been assigned this mountain to show others it can be moved." – Unknown

By now, you realize people are in two categories: those who are looking and those who are watching. Specifically, those looking to see if the change that has come over you will stick and those watching to see if you can maintain your composure during this time of trial and tribulation.

A mountain is a stone and try as you might, when you beat on it, you cannot get blood from it. However, you will get gravel, so here it is: no matter what form the mountain takes, be it, a man or woman, your job, a lie, or the truth, you must operate from your new position of strength. The next mountain to get in your way will be pulverized into gravel.

Gone are the days of lack and squeezing blood from stones. We are in the gravel making business now and we are celebrating joy by the pound. This is going to be a good week. Don't let anything get in your way. You already know the mountain is going to move, so let's get out our hammer and begin beating the mountain into submission. No more being weighed down by lack, fools, and desperation. You are now busting stone into gravel.

Scripture of the day: Psalm 92:4
"For you Lord have made me glad through your work; I will triumph in the works of your hands."

Day 37: Own This Day

"Make sure you don't start seeing yourself through the eyes of those who don't value you. Know your worth, even if they don't." – Thema Davis

Your assignment – if you choose to accept – is:
1. To believe in yourself
2. Know that your words matter
3. Know that the power you possess makes you strong and more capable to overcome any obstacle

Traps have been set to hinder and frustrate you, so be aware of the hindrances as they may be disguised as a change of heart or a one-sided favor. Remember, they have never liked you and have belittled your value.

You've been out in the world and your skills are much improved. You are stronger, a wiser, and you understand your value better now. The world has been waiting for you. We need you – your team needs you. Right now, say this to yourself:

I am valuable. I love me. I will own this day.

Go out and own this day.

Scripture of the day: Mark 9:23
"Jesus said unto him, 'If you can believe, all things are possible to him that believes.'"

Day 38: Sunshine Mixed with a Little Hurricane

"A woman is the full circle. Within her is the power to create, nurture and transform." – Diane Mariechild

No man's life is ever the same once he has come in contact with a woman. Every room she enters is forever changed by her presence, voice, and beauty. Try as we might to ignore her, men must pay attention to her. Whenever she walks into a room, men become their six-year-old selves; showing off just to get her to look in our direction for just a momentary glance of recognition.

The power within a woman is both electrifying and smooth reminiscent of "sunshine mixed with a little hurricane" a ball of swirling effervescent energy and strength that can make a child giddy with anticipation for a hug, and a grown man long for her flavor.

She's so smart; that she has to hide it because the male ego at times is the very eggshells she must walk on. She has the power to create laughter and make a man want to be better. Little girls want to be her, walk like her, talk like her.

Yet, if you wrong her, the hurricane swirls silently churning building energy that once released, surely will transform your mind. Resting in her eyes is the warmth and calmness of the sun, but the outer edges will rip you to shreds for simply coming at her the wrong way. A woman is the crowded circle and within her is the power to nurture and transform.

Scripture of the day: Proverbs 22:1
"A good name is rather to be chosen than great riches, and loving favor rather than silver and gold."

Day 39: You Are the Difference Maker

"Remember: You are a different person now than before. You are wiser and stronger for the trials that you have been through." – Leon Brown

Your lights are on, and yes, that is you – it's your voice; you look different and feel different, and it hasn't been long at all, but you've changed. It's time to embrace the fact: you are different, you have always been different, it's okay to be different, and I like you being different.

Your newly found difference comes with responsibility. No more playing small so others can feel good around you. Your thinking must be bold and solution-based. Your words have power and what you say to people matters. Anger is a suit that does not fit you well, therefore improve your arguments.

Remember, you are smarter than you were before – you have earned every bit of the wisdom your work, loving, and living experiences have taught you. Gone are the days of "*I don't know why I like it, but I do*" decision-making. You have always been smart.

Scripture of the Day: Job 31:6
"Let me be weighed on honest scales, that God may know my integrity."

Day 40: You Are a Superhero

Okay, listen – we've made it through another day. You've survived every trap, you've overcome every illness, and you've killed every bad attitude with kindness. You have conquered your mountain and destroyed all doubt that you had about your capabilities, so here's what I need you to do. Put your hands on your waist, do your best superhero pose, and say this aloud:

I know who I am; I am strong, smart, courageous, and free! Let there be no doubt – I dig me! There is no one like me!

The victory is yours today!

Scripture of the day: Proverbs 23:7
"For as he thinks in his heart, so is he."

Day 41: Make Yourself a Priority

"It's not selfish to love yourself, take care of yourself, and to make your happiness a priority. It's a necessity." – Mandy Hale

The change that has come over you – this new found assertive dominance you display takes a lot out of you. You find yourself pleased with your daily accomplishments but utterly worn out at the end of the week.

That's good! You are a good warrior as you have discovered your proper preparation allows you to win the mental game in advance and dominate the physical realm with your presence. Just as you know, you cannot run wide open without taking your foot off the internal throttle to rest and recuperate your body, mind, and spirit. It's necessary.

Love yourself, take care of yourself, and make yourself a priority today.

Scripture of the day: Psalm 16:9
"Therefore my heart is glad and my glory rejoices: my flesh also will rest in hope."

Day 42: You Can and Must Save Your Own World

So it's come to this – your world needs saving and you are the only person with the skills to turn back your enemies. Before you depart for your mission, there are two critical pieces of information you must have: (1) You are a one-man army and (2) Ain't no help coming.

You will need to use each of the new skills you have been developing during your journey and let the following serve as your reminder of your ability:

1. Your courage is unmatched. You possess a new bravery and willingness to fight that you didn't know you had when we started out.
2. You are a smart, multi-tasking, problem-solving beast!
3. Your patience has become amazing; You have learned to silently wait out your prey before you strike.
4. Your assertive dominance has replaced your rage.

As you get out into the field, watch for the passive aggressive attacks. Know this and understand that all insurrections must be put down.

As a one-man army you fight with no rules – only sports have rules and your life ain't no game. Check your gear: Belt of truth? Check. Breastplate of righteousness? Check. Feet fitted with readiness? Check. Shield of faith? Check. Helmet of salvation? Check. The Sword of the Spirit? Check.

Now go and save your world.

Scripture of the day: Philippians 3:14
"I press toward the goal for the prize of the upward call of God in Christ Jesus."

Day 43: Find the Nerve

"Anything's possible if you got enough nerve." – J.K. Rowling

What is it that you have wanted to do but have been afraid to take the chance? Most of us have these things we want to try, but up until now, we have not had the nerve. I think one of the problems, at least for me, is that I would retreat back into my comfort zone. The thing about comfort zones is that the things you hold dear and deem important get lost in the darkness of your comfort zone, like your passion, dreams, vision and time.

It's a good thing we've found our way out of the comfort zone and moved out to the deep water. So here's your new challenge for today. Make a list of three things you have been wanting to do, but never had enough nerve to get done.

Now, I want to introduce you to a new term I learned from Stacey, my wife: "uncomfortable change". Your list must require you to make an uncomfortable change and remember the above quote. Now keep in mind, you don't have to make the changes all at once and if you need help, ask for it.

Let's continue to break free from our comfort zones. You are a mountain mover who continues to move out into the deep water.

It's time to do what you've been wanting to do.

Scripture of the day: 2 Timothy 1:7
"For God has not given us a spirit of fear, but of power and of love and of a sound mind."

Day 44: Go on Girl, Be Your Own Hero

"She became dangerous to them when she no longer needed or cared for their approval." – JM Storm

It's amazing, the freedom that a woman obtains when she is no longer fearful. She's free to do, be and explore the world and create something new.

Scripture of the Day: Isaiah 54:2
"Enlarge the place of your tent, and let them stretch out the curtains of your dwellings; Do not spare; Lengthen your cords, and strengthen your stakes."

Day 45: Rock on Warrior, Rock On.

"Whether it's a sucker punch or you saw it coming, you still got punched." – Mark Corbin

Try as you might to call it something else – that was *not* a sucker punch. No, you didn't see if coming, but at this point, you should expect any and everything that gets thrown your way. No, they are not there to help you, no, they are not there to encourage you, and no, they will not apologize when you catch them doing you wrong. Well, mountain mover, let's take the easy solutions off the table – no crushing, no destroying, and definitely no '*I will get you and your dog Todo too*'. Yes, those are easy for the average person, but you have not been average for some time; you are a warrior now! That's why the knock down did not hurt you. You are strong and tougher now. So say this aloud: *this is why I train.*

We train to learn out limits, physical as well as mental and emotional, keeping in mind that getting knocked down is only a problem if you stay down. That is what our training has been about – finding out what you can take.

It was a good shot; a punch like that six months ago would have crippled the old you, but it's a new season and you are a mountain-moving warrior. Now, you know what you can take. It's a different fight now isn't it? Assertive domination is the path, deep water is the goal, and fighting honorably and hitting hard is the way.

Take a good look at yourself and smile. You're looking good and feeling good. I know we forgot who we were for a while, but welcome back – the world has been waiting for you.

Scripture of the day: Psalm 30:11
"You have turned for me my mourning into dancing..."

Day 46: Be Bold Today.

"Behind me is infinite power. Before me endless possibility, and around me is boundless opportunity." – Mac Anderson

So you have arrived at this day in your life alive and well. Every day before today has served as a battery, a way to store energy to be used by you to grow, to succeed and to thrive. Far too many days and nights have passed that you have not been satisfied with the results of how you have lived your life, but today will not be like any other day; your power is no longer stored up! Your power has a point of discharge now. You have identified your future destinations and possibilities of your love and success.

The world has been waiting for you to display your infinite power, to show us what is possible, and to lead us into boundless opportunities that lay before us. Now let go and release that stored energy. The world is waiting for you.

Scripture of the day: 3 John 2
"Beloved, I pray that you may prosper in all things and be in health, just as your soul prospers."

Day 47: Rest Well.

"Celebrate what you've accomplished, but raise the bar a little higher each time you succeed." – Mia Hamm

Well mountain-moving warrior, you made it to another day a little beaten but definitely better for having gone through the struggles of yesterday. Today, we rest and review our list of boundless opportunities that we have written down. Review your list as now it's time to think about strategy. Grab a sheet of paper and on one side, create a list of goals. On the other side, create a list of strategies to accomplish your goals. Do this right away. On the right margin, write out the 5Ws – *Who, What, When, Where,* and *Why.* Every day, we will work one of the 5Ws.

Enjoy your day and continue to raise the bar each day.

Scripture of the day: Genesis 24:40
"But he said to me, 'The Lord, before whom I walk, will send His angel with you and prosper your way; and you shall take a wife for my son from my family and from my father's house."

Day 48: Who

"Sometimes there is no next time, no second chance, no time out. Sometimes it's just now or never." – Alan Bennett

No more waiting and no more asking for permission. Right now is your time. Do not wait for them to come along and say it's okay for you to be you. This is a ride you will take by yourself. You will not be alone – the mountain-moving warriors are with you. Tomorrow is still going to come whether you take action today or not.

WHO: *Write down your full name, who you are (mother, sister, brother, father, etc.), and your occupation. Then write down what you dreamt you would be as a child, then who you will be at the end of this year, and how you will change.*

Make this fun – consider how much sweeter and how strong you will feel because you decided to change and take action on your behalf. This is it – there is no tapping out, no quitting, and no mind changing.

It's now or never. It's not simple, but it is one foot in front of the other. You've got to firmly grab the life you want with both hands and squeeze and pull it into existence inch by inch. This is the dawning of your new day so stand up right now with your arms opened wide and greet the day.

This is your day now. Go get what's yours.

Scripture of the day: Isaiah 30:21
"Your ears shall hear a word behind you, saying, 'this is the way, walk in it,' whenever you turn to the right hand or whenever you turn to the left."

Day 49: Don't Turn Your Back

"It doesn't matter how this looks to other people. If this is something you gotta do, then you do it. Fighters fight." – Rocky Balboa

Each day you wake and prepare yourself to attack your day and obstacles that stand in the way of you having what it is you want. You get up and keep going because there is no other choice for you. Stopping is not an option? If you stop, you die. You can't settle anymore. Yes, each day looks hard, but it doesn't matter how it looks to other people. This is *your* life and if it were easy, someone else would be living it.

This is *your* life – you must prepare to fight for it. Put your breast plate on right now and fasten the sides firmly. We are only moving forward from here. The breast plate will stop the slings and arrows that get thrown at your heart and the lies and whining that have been conceived to make you stop. You fight forward because this is what you must do for you.

So yes, fight, one step at a time if you must, but each of those steps is forward, never back. That is why your back is not covered – because you are not going that way. Those voices off in the distance that echo in your ear will slowly fade and you will no longer hear them calling you, telling you to *"stay here (where I can control you)"* or *"we are good together (because you do what I say)"*. Face your future and move forward.

Don't you dare turn your back on your life. Now get up and do what you have to do! Fighters fight!

Scripture of the day: Psalm 119:105
"Thy word is a lamp to my feet and a light to my path."

WHAT: Write down the three things from your opportunity list. What are you willing to do to achieve your goal? Make a list of people who can help you.

Day 50: Do You Hear What I Hear?

"One of the most beautiful sounds that I have ever heard is the sound of a beautiful, strong woman's voice once she's discovered her true worth. She sounds empowered... she sounds confident... but most of all, she sounds free." – Amari Soul

When in the presence of a woman, you can get lost looking at her. It is not what you see that holds your attention, it's the longing to hear her voice speak to you. It's not that she calls your name, it's the way the words are ushered through her lips. You can hear that subtle power layered underneath of her tone. Her tone grabs and directs you where she wants you to be. As you watch her speak her mind, you are stuck between beauty and power knowing she has discovered that she is finally in control. She is free.

Knowing her power is one thing, but once a woman understands her true worth, it is a sight to behold. Mothers, sisters, and daughters who know their value will tell you what you just learned – that she has always been confident, strong and free.

Scripture of the day: Psalm 143:10
"Teach me to do Your will, for You are my God; your Spirit is good. Lead me in the land of uprightness."

WHEN: You must be specific regarding your start and end date of your project or change. Do not use phrases like "this year" – be specific about your date.

Day 51: I Choose to Fight!

"Nobody is born a warrior. You choose to be one when you refuse to stay seated. You choose to be one when you refuse to back down. You choose to be one when you stand up after getting knocked down. You choose to be one because if not you, who?" – Being Caballero

"You came into this world kicking and screaming and covered in someone else's blood." The fact of the matter is you are willing to leave this world the same way if the need should arise.

You have chosen to be a warrior because you refuse to stay seated in the face of apathy and injustice you witness each day. You are a warrior because you have chosen to help those who cannot fight for themselves. People see you smile and they think they know you and believe you are a calm soul who will take their insults and stand in their shade.

You have never been someone's punching bag or doormat. You have been knocked down and have gotten back up again and again. You are a warrior! The time has come to fight. So, here it is: today take a step on the path of assertive domination, step forward and tell the world why you came here. You came to fight!

Scripture of the day: Psalm 91:10
"No evil shall befall you, nor shall any plague come near your dwelling."

WHERE: Where will you live? Where will you fight for your life? Choose your battle ground and fight.

Day 52: Let Nothing Stand in Your Way.

Warriors Creed:
Honesty; always be true to myself, stand for virtue.
Humility; acknowledge weaknesses, never flaunt my strength
Control of Power; never abuse that which I have learned, always be aware
Courage; face my fears, acknowledge them, stand tall facing danger
Concentration; invoke the strength of body, mind, and spirit
Endurance; focus and training is my stability, strong and powerful is my body, and my spirit is my drive

Are you strong? Yes. Are you smart? Yes. Is there anything that can keep you from your success? No. Are you ready? Yes. Will you win today? Yes.

You are prepared you are a mountain-moving warrior. There is no need to be afraid; you came to fight and you came to win. Show no mercy today and do what you have to do.

Scripture of the day: 1 Peter 5:7
"Casting all your care upon Him, for He cares for you."

WHY: The *why* should be more than money.

Day 53: Set That Fire Down Inside Today.

"Attitude is everything. New strength, new day, new strength, and new thoughts." – Unknown

Another killer day down, and just so you know, people are watching. This is what they will think when they see you today:

"I like the way you wear your hair – I like the stylish clothes you wear – it's just the little things you do – that show me how much you care."

Peace and love, don't push and shove – unless you have to.

Scripture of the day: James 3:18
"And the fruit of righteousness is sown in peace by those who make peace."

Day 54: This Battle I Will Win

"I am a warrior. This is war. This is a battle I will win." – Unknown

On this morning, the call has gone out and the trumpet has sounded. A new day has come and all enemies must be put down. The timid fear this day, but not you. This is no ordinary day – this is Black Flag Day. Today you will fight in the hall on the street in the dirt and thistle to defeat the enemy. You have seen this enemy before and you know all too well that it leaves in its wake apathy, sin, lust, anger, evil, and disobedience. Indeed, the call has gone out at the trumpets sound and only my warrior brethren have answered the call. They have arrived alone and together the old man, the preacher, the counselor, the striker along with the power, and the glory, forged in the jungle, tested in the city, the arena and the committee. As I look to my left and to my right and then to the horizon, I have but one thought for those who would get in my way – *May God's grace be sufficient for you.'*

I fight for my future, fierce, strong, and ever ready. For on this day, I offer no peace and surrender is unacceptable.

This is a battle I will win.

Scripture of the day: Psalm 78:38
"But He, being full of compassion, forgave their iniquity, and did not destroy them. Yes, many a time He turned His anger away, and did not stir up all His wrath."

Day 55: It's Starting to Rain

"If you're gonna fight, fight like you're the third monkey on the ramp to Noah's Ark... and brother, it's starting to rain."
– Unknown

There is no need to stand there looking at the door. Yep, *they* are on the other side waiting on you and for a moment, you almost feel sorry for them, but alas, that moment has passed. You did all that you could not enter this battle. You walked around the long way and even showed deference to their process and position, but they chose to have no appreciation for your calm. They have chosen to stand on your path and to get in the way of what you have claimed in Jesus name.

So be it. If war is what they want, war is what they will get. And just in case you forgot how precarious the situation is. keep in mind the following: you are the third monkey on the ramp to Noah's Ark and brother, it's starting to rain.

Scripture of the day: Proverbs 16:20
"He who heeds the word wisely will find good, and whoever trusts in the Lord, happy is he."

Day 56: She's Bad

"She's a badass with a good heart, soft but strong. Unapologetic and honest. She's the type of woman you go to war beside; the type of woman you marry." – R.H. Sin

There is nothing more to say.

Scripture of the day: Jeremiah 29:11
"For I know the thoughts that I think toward you, says the Lord, thoughts of peace and not of evil, to give you a future and a hope."

Day 57: Whatever It Takes

"Remember that the reason you are doing this is to make your life better." – Unknown

Every morning you wake before the alarm sounds – not to be early, but because you are ready; ready to do whatever is required of you to have what you claim. Let's check the list:

1. Prayer – check.
2. Sacrifice – check.
3. Reach exceeding your grasp – check.
4. Barriers moved, gone over, or destroyed – check, check, and check.

Making your life better is serious business, so when the sun rises and you look into the mirror today, ask yourself this question: What must I do to make my life better? Look back at your reflection of yourself, smile, and say, "Whatever it takes."

Scripture of the day: Philippians 4:13
"I can do all things through Christ who strengthens me."

Day 58: Do It Well or Don't Do It at All

"To be nobody but yourself in a world that's doing its best to make you somebody else, is to fight the hardest battle you are ever going to fight. Never stop fighting." – E.E. Cummings

By now, you clearly understand the square peg does not fit in the round hole, that objects in the mirror are closer than they appear, and there is a reason no one talks about the other four smooth stones. Each and every day you work at remaining relevant in a world that does not understand your value. There are days when you convince yourself that those people and that place need you, but keep in mind that the one morning you wake up and find yourself dead, is the day they will find someone to replace you.

Truth be told you know who you are – ain't no need holding back now. It doesn't even feel comfortable anymore, pretending you don't know the answers so they can feel better about themselves.

Listen to the great McFadden & Whitehead song "Ain't No Stopping Us Now:'

Ain't no stopping me now, I am on the move. There is nothing that can stand in my way. I have put myself together and polished up my act. There is nothing that can stand in my way.

Scripture of the day: Psalm 38:9a
"Lord, all my desire is before you…"

Day 59: Have A Good Time.

"Moon dust in your lungs, stars in your eyes, you are a child of the cosmos – a ruler of the skies." – Emma Roeske

It's time to cut loose and in the words of DJ Kool:

"I just came to party, to dance, and have a good time.
I don't really care if ya'll don't have a good time.
I'm gonna do my thing; I'm gone have a good time.
I don't really need you just to have a good time."

Scripture of the day: Lamentations 3:25
"The Lord is good to those who wait for Him, to the soul that seeks Him."

Day 60: Those Days Are Gone

"Someone once told me not to bite off more than I can chew; I said I'd rather choke on greatness than nibble on mediocrity." – Unknown

It is time to rock and roll – this is greatness week! Your assignment is plain and simple: you must bite off more than you can chew. Your reach must exceed your grasp and you must do more than you thought you were capable of.

No more being bent over tired, cold, and thirsty while eating out of the trough of mediocrity. Listen, you can have all that you claim but first determine what you want, when you want it, and how bad you want it. Once you figured out what you want then you MUST determine who you can help achieve their goals.

The only way for you and I to grow is to help someone else grow.

Gone are the days of nibbling at the edges of the wanton plate of mediocrity. We have come here to feast upon the greatness of the promises of God.

Now, step up to the table, pull out your chair, sit down, and give thanks for His goodness.

Scripture of the day: Proverbs 3:2
"For length of days and long life and peace they will add to you."

71

Day 61: You've Got Big Things to Do!

"It's time to stop pretending you're this average person. You've got big things to do – BIG!" – Tiffany Han

Let's start here – you are not average and you have never been average. I know you find it hard to believe, I get it. Average is all you can ever strive for if that's all you have ever known – sort of like Cinderella having to sneak into the ball with her fly gear on and having to sneak out before her carriage turns into a pumpkin.

But to hell with that – we ain't sneaking in and we ain't running out. We are taking these glass slippers off this year. This year, we are turning around, going back into that room and beating the boots off of anybody who gets in our way.

So, you hold your head up high and tell them out loud: *I am great and nothing or nobody shall stand in our way!*

Scripture of the day: Psalm 37:5
"Commit your way unto the Lord; trust also in Him; and He shall bring it to pass."

Day 62: R-E-S-P-E-C-T – Now You Know

"Truly powerful women don't explain why they want respect. They simple don't engage those who don't give it to them." – Sherry Argov

We are now living in an age where women know their value and capabilities, so let this be a warning – you may not know who she is when she walks into a room and you may not know what to say, but you should think the following: R-E-S-P-E-C-T and let her walk on by.

Scripture of the day: Galatians 6:9
"And let us not grow weary while doing good, for in due season we shall reap if we do not lose heart."

Day 63: I Am Great!

"Be not afraid of greatness. Some are born great, some achieve greatness, and some have greatness thrust upon them." – William Shakespeare

You have known all of your life that you are different. You have been made to feel uncomfortable about your differentness. You realized that you were smarter than some, tougher than others, and you even tried to hide your differentness just to keep your friends. All these years you've been trying to figure out what this thing is that's been hanging around you.

Well let me be the first to tell you, it's greatness and it has been with you all along. The first step into greatness is acceptance.

Having greatness thrust upon you can be a shock, but now that you know who you are and what that feeling you've been carrying around inside of you is, your smile will be so big and bright that some folks might not recognize you.

You are ready.
You are capable.
You are enough.
You've got big things to do.

Scripture of the day: Psalm 84:11
"For the Lord God is a sun and shield; the Lord will give grace and glory; no good thing will He withhold from those who walk uprightly."

Day 64: Buckle Up, It's Going to Be a Great Ride

"Surround yourself with the dreamers and the doers, the believers and thinkers, but most of all, surround yourself with those who see greatness within you, even when you don't see it yourself." – Edmund Lee

It's a new day. Now that you have embraced your greatness, it's time to put your greatness squad together. Think carefully about who will fill the roles of dreamers, doers, believers, thinkers, and those who believe in you.

Now, the people on your greatness squad must be people who are not afraid of you. Your greatness squad must consist of those who will tell you the truth and most importantly, you must be willing to listen.

You are great – embrace that fact. Life will be different from here. It's going to be a great ride, so buckle up.

Scripture of the day: Philippians 1:6
"Being confident of this very thing, that He who has begun a good work in you will perform it until the day of Jesus Christ."

Day 65: You Are Amazing

"In case you forgot to remind yourself this morning – you are beautiful. Your smile lights up a room, your mind is amazing, and you are much cooler than you think. You are more than enough and you are doing an amazing job at life."
– Unknown

You continue to surpass your former self. Congratulations. Let's continue to raise and bend the bar.

Scripture of the day: Proverbs 3:13
"Happy is the man who finds wisdom, and the man who gains understanding."

Day 66: Come on And Do Your Thing

"Do your thing. Do it unapologetically. Don't be discouraged by criticism. You probably already know what they're going to say. Pay no mind to the fear of failure. It's far more valuable than success. Take ownership, take chances, and have fun. And no matter what, don't ever stop doing your thing." – Asher Roth

The time has finally come – it's time to do your thing! Don't be concerned about failure. Only the brave and courageous and those in the arena fail. You cannot fail sitting on the couch. You do not know what you are capable of if you never try.

There is no losing, there is only learning. Learn from your efforts, great and small. Take ownership of your efforts and remove "sorry" from your vocabulary.

Take a risk and no matter what comes your way this week, do your thing.

Scripture of the day: Philippians 3:14
"I press toward the goal for the prize of the upward calling of God in Christ Jesus."

Day 67: That's Your Greatness Knocking

"The one thing nobody else has is you. Your voice, your mind, your story, your vision. So write and draw and build and play and dance and live only as you can." – Neil Gaiman

You can search the whole world over and never find someone like you. When enemies appear and friends disappear, all you have is you. Your voice is the voice that will give your victory yell. Your mind will be the creator of the dynamic strategy that will ultimately get you out of harm's way. You will be the teller of your story of foes defeated and victories won. It is your vision that will cut a path through the haze of those who try to murky the waters with foolishness in order to appear deep.

So, write your future bold and bright and declare this day how great you are. Draw up a plan and build your reputation upon truth and honor, respect for your foes, and fear no one.

Find the passion of your youth; find your theme song and dance your dance. All of creation is waiting on you so come out here and share your greatness with the world.

This life won't work without you.

Scripture of the day: Mark 9:23
"Jesus said to him, 'If you can believe, all things are possible to him who believes.'"

Day 68: Fight Girl, Fight

"She was a true fighter, you could see it in her eyes. She was not born strong; she was made strong. She was sculpted to be her own hero when the world let her down, and she kept picking herself back up." – Arpita Chatterjee

Women are strong because they must be. She has power so intense that it must be tempered because its full release is misunderstood by friends and foes alike. She has eyes that pierce the soul and eyes that cry tears that wash away the stain of loneliness, boredom, years of tiredness and duplicitous behaviors of weak lovers.

Mythical heroes are created on Mount Olympus, but not her – she was sculpted to be her own hero on the streets and hallways everywhere, including her own home. She does not need your cheers because she brings her own. She cares little for your Amen because she brings her own. She has what she needs to get up when she gets knocked down. She's a grown woman who wears a crown and holds her head high as she displays her majesty and might, but here's a warning: *"it's not the size of the girl in the fight, it's the size of the fight in the girl."*

Scripture of the day: Proverbs 13:9a
"The light of the righteous rejoices..."

Day 69: Fix Your Attitude

"A bad attitude can literally block love, blessings, and destiny from finding you. Don't be the reason you don't succeed." – Mandy Hale

If the only thing keeping you happy is a smile, then why don't you smile? Don't not smile because of your interaction with someone else. Don't allow yourself to be pushed to the highest level of "pisstivity" by someone who does not have your best interest at heart.

Fix your attitude, turn that frown upside down, and smile. Smile as if your life depended on it. It's time to give up frowning and that unfriendly nature of yours. It takes 12 muscles to frown and 11 to smile – see, even math is in your favor. Stop blocking your future favor with a bad attitude – it is that simple.

Some people will be afraid of the smiling you, but if they're going to be scared of you, it might as well be because they don't know what your smile really means.

Scripture of the day: Galatians 6:9
"And let us not grow weary while doing good, for in due season we shall reap if we do not lose heart."

Day 70: The Fight Continues

"Never be afraid to fail. Never give up because F.A.I.L. is an acronym for First Attempt In Learning." – Unknown

It's been a good, long journey and you are learning and winning. It's great to discover new strengths as we continue to ply our trade, love our family, and start strengthening and growing relationships. We need to adjust our mindset away from the permanence of failure. What I mean is that just because it did not go your way, does not mean don't ever try again. Go back and analyze your behavior and interactions and change what you can for the next opportunity.

You see, winning comes by doing, practicing, and learning a little bit each day. You win in the arena, not the day of the game. You win on all the days of doing, failing, and learning in practice. To be great is not a show-up-and-win kind of thing; you win the trophy long before the day the fight starts, so keep in mind that our day in the arena is coming. We are learning well in our first attempts in learning. Learn well warrior, as the fight is real and it continues.

Scripture of the day: John 10:10

"The thief does not come except to steal, and to kill, and to destroy. I have come that they may have life, and that they may have it more abundantly."

Day 71: Keep Doing What You're Doing

"Remember how far you've come, not just how far you have to go. You are not where you want to be, but neither are you where you used to be." – Rick Warren

One of the tough things about being us is that we tend to believe that we never accomplish anything meaningful. Now you can use your own language around the strategy, but my purpose today is to assure you that you are doing fine.

Scripture of the day: Lamentations 3:25
"The Lord is good to those who wait for Him, to the soul who seeks Him."

Day 72: Are You Ready?

"Stay afraid, but do it anyway. What's important is the action. You don't have to wait to be confident. Just do it and eventually the confidence will follow." – Carrie Fisher

Whenever you decide to change, there is a certain amount of fear and trepidation. Fear and trepidation are one in the same the thing. So, why be afraid of a thing twice as much when it cannot harm you but once?

We are born with two fear responses and they are falling and loud noises – neither of those two things can impede a person's success. Surely, you can trip and fall and some people love to yell at you, but you cannot spend all of your time in a perpetual state of looking for things that will make you fall or walking around with your fingers in your ears to keep out the noise.

Ditch the fear and take your fingers out of your ears and boldly take action to live, find and kick the door open into a new life, love or career that is searching for you to find it.

Listen and understand that you are the personification of greatness. Yes, you! So, I have one question for you: Are you ready?

Scripture of the day: Proverbs 3:6
"In all your ways acknowledge Him, and He shall direct your paths."

Day 73: Be the Best that Ever Did It

"At the end of the day, you gotta feel some way. So why not feel unbeatable? Why not feel untouchable? Why not feel like the best to ever do it?" – Conor McGregor

If you could go back in time and choose to relive the best day of your life all over again, in one word, how did you feel at the end of that day? Now you understand the premise of this quote. You don't have a time machine; you cannot go back in time to relive a day that will never come again, so decide right now – how will you feel at the end of this day?

Today you have three new choices. You will be unbeatable – no man, woman or job will beat you today. You will be untouchable and no weapon formed against you shall proper, no arrow and no subversive plot will succeed against you this day.

So, declare this day that you are the best to ever do it. Certainly, there will be those standing around looking, watching and waiting for you to fall, but do not despair – the reason they are all waiting is that they are all trying to figure who is coming in second.

Scripture of the Day: 2 Kings 6:16
"So he answered, 'Do not fear, for those who are with us are more than those who are with them.'"

Day 74: He Doesn't Move Until You Breath

"Take a deep breath and remember who you are!" – Maya Knowles

Breathing is fundamental to life and without it, there is no living. Dear lady, always remember that every child's first breath is because of you. There is a man somewhere whose breath you have taken away by just walking into the room. There have been entire businesses that have held their combined breath because they have feared your wrath.

So girl, listen: the next time you find yourself flustered, angry, doubtful, or lost, take a deep breath and remember who you are. You are a life giver, breath taker and a world maker. Keep this tucked away in the back of your mind. This life isn't worth living without you.

Scripture of the day: Romans 11:29
"For the gifts and the calling of God are irrevocable."

Day 75: Work On Your Plan Everyday

"Decide what you want, make a plan and work on it every single day." – Unknown

Do not lose sight of what is important, but first, be clear about what is important to you and remember that not everything is important. My best friend says make the plan, write the plan, and work the plan.

Work the plan every day and do not be afraid to do the little things every day to get better. Pray, be humble, be kind, help others, be respectful, do something physical with your body, and drink water. You can make your own list, but know who you are and where the people you are related to come from. This knowledge is important because they will always be with you.

You are on the right path, so decide what you want, make a plan, and work on it every single day.

Scripture of the day: Proverbs 16:20
"He who heeds the word wisely will find good, and whoever trusts in the Lord, happy is he."

Day 76: Ignore Your Limits by Taking One Step Forward

"All men have limits. They learn what they are and learn not to exceed them. I ignore mine." – Batman

Once your mind, heart, and soul are exposed to something new, it is changed forever. Most of us are taught to stay in front of the house, to stay in our lane, and that things come to those who wait. We are taught to limit ourselves for our own protection, but nothing great was ever accomplished by not crossing the line. The history of the world would be vastly different if every person that died today had taken action and exceeded their limits.

Let me tell you about yourself – we are 76 days into this battle together and you have learned to fight and you realized you are much stronger than you thought. Now it is time to boldly go into the future taking even bigger steps towards your blessings and greatness. Listen, if you take just one step forward with humility and self-confidence, know that you have gone further than ever before. One bold step each day is all it takes to exceed your limits.

Scripture of the day: Psalm 91:10
"No evil shall befall you, nor shall any plague come near your dwelling."

Day 77: We've Got Some Things to Prove to Ourselves

"Commitment means staying loyal to what you said you were going to do long after the mood you said it in has left you." – Unknown

Only do what you are capable of doing.

Scripture of the day: Deuteronomy 29:9
"Therefore keep the words of this covenant, and do them, that you may prosper in all that you do."

Day 78: Get Ready -- Stay Ready

"Every time you train, train with the motivation and purpose that you will be the hardest person someone ever tries to kill." – Tim Kennedy

Train your mind.

Train your body.

Train your children.

The day will come when the proverbial "IT" will come after you. If you are not ready, you won't need to get ready.

Scripture of the day: 3 John 2
"Beloved, I pray that you may prosper in all things and be in health, just as your soul prospers."

Day 79: A Gentleman's Checklist

"A gentleman will open doors, pull out chairs, and carry things, not because you are helpless and unable, but because he wants to show you that you are valuable and worthy of respect." – Unknown

Okay ladies, here's the checklist:

1. Open the door? Check.
2. Pull out your chair? Check.
3. Carry what needs to be carried. Check.
4. Respect your opinion even if he disagrees? Check.
5. Know where he needs to stand in love mode, respect mode, and protect mode. Check, check and check.

He values, respects and can listen to you. If you got that, then together, you can make your world go round.

Scripture of the day: Colossians 3:13a
"Bearing with one another, and forgiving one another, if anyone has a complaint against another; even as Christ forgave you, so you also must do."

Day 80: Your Time is Coming

"There comes a time when one must take a position that is neither safe nor political, nor popular, but he must take it because conscience tells him it is right." – Martin Luther King Jr.

Your time is coming.

Scripture of the day: Proverbs 16:3
"Commit your works to the Lord and your thoughts will be established."

Day 81: You in or Out?

"When you look in the mirror and see no change, and still keep faith, knowing that in time, you will get there if you stay focused, that's the difference between those who succeed and those who fail." – Unknown

I am glad you are awake and well. Today is a new day and we got things to do. What three things do you most need to accomplish today? Which three people must you talk to with today? What three goals must be worked on today?

No more average days. Life has changed and you need you to make a decision. Are you in or out?

Scripture of the day: Psalm 35:9
"And my soul shall be joyful in the Lord; it shall rejoice in His salvation."

Day 82: Are Your Bags Packed?

"When God gives you a vision, you will be able to discern between the people in your life who are equipped for the journey, and those who forgot to pack." – Minister Donald Graham

Your journey is not for everybody, so stop trying to take people with you who do not really want to go or belong on the journey. What God has for you is not for Joe-Joe and his friends, so stop calling him. The time has come to embrace your greatness, blessings, and the grace you have been given and walk in it.

Your vision ain't for everybody to see – that's why it's your vision. Those who forgot to pack ain't going, so stop fooling around with them. One day, the trumpet will sound, don't get caught standing around with Joe-Joe and those other jokers talking about, "Did ya'll hear that? That ain't what I thought it was?"

Scripture of the day: Deuteronomy 4:29
"But from there you will seek the Lord your God and you will find Him if you seek Him with all your heart and with all your soul."

Day 83: Stronger Than Before

"In the end you'll see you won't stop me." – Christina Aguilera

They thought they could stop you with their tricks, guile and cunning, but little did they know that you are going to get out – even if you have to crawl out. You will crawl out stronger.

It's another day and you did it again. Beat them until they couldn't take anymore. The enemy forgot that you don't quit and that you fight, we win.

Scripture of the day: Zechariah 4:6b
"'Not by might nor by power, but by my spirit,' says the Lord of hosts."

Day 84: Courage Fills My Cup

"If there is one thing you've got to hold onto, it's the courage to fight." – Unknown

Once you learn how to fight, the desire to fight subsides. You continue to train in order to remain a violent and lethal weapon, but what happens is you discover how dangerous you have become. The courage to fight never goes away; it's ever present and remains a sweet taste in your mouth. That's why you pity the fool who pushes you to fight – they don't recognize that once you uncork your fight genie from the bottle there is no way it will go back in.

Fill your cup with courage this morning because ready or not, the fight is coming.

Scripture of the day: Romans 8:31
"What then shall we say in response to these things? If God is for us, who can be against us?"

Day 85: Stacey – Sparked the Revolution

"Your soulmate is not someone that comes into your life peacefully. It is who comes to make you question things, who changes reality, somebody that marks a before and after in your life. It is not the human being everyone idealized, but an ordinary person, who manages to revolutionize your world in a second." – Anonymous

For me, the revolution has started and it is being lived live and in living color.

Scripture of the day: Psalm 144:15
"Happy are the people who are in such a state; happy are the people whose God is the Lord."

Day 86: Right, Straight and Strong

"Trying to keep my mind right, my soul straight, and my heart strong." – Unknown

Each and every day you rise, you must be prepared to fight and enlarge your territory, keeping your mind focused and your soul straight just to keep from throat punching people who think that it is there duty to test you.

Keep praying and praising God, tend to your soul's care daily, love hard, and love who you want. Trying to keep your mind right and your soul straight is a daily task, but thanks be unto God for Jesus.

Scripture of the Day: Proverbs 3:26
"For the Lord will be your confidence, and will keep your foot from being caught."

Day 87: You Are Enough – Set Yourself Free

"The most important day is the day you decide you're good enough for you. It's the day you set yourself free." – Brittany Josephina

No more gilded cages and no more people pleasing. This is your life – live it like it deserves to be lived. It's time to snatch the door off the hinges of the box you've been existing in. Your existence has been about being and being is not living. You want proof, then dig this: if you died tomorrow, the only thing that would be left in the unremarkable cage you have been living in would be nothing because even the paper lining the bottom of the cage would be thrown out.

Decide today that you are good enough for you. You have always been good enough, and most days, even better. I believe you can fly and it's time to spread your wings and soar.

Scripture of the day: Proverbs 3:13
"Happy is the man who finds wisdom and the man who gains understanding."

Day 88: The Party is Over

"Everything you are going through is preparing you for everything you asked." – Unknown

The party is over – the pity party you've been quietly having. I know you needed that moment – I've had mine and I get it. So, you have been getting your butt kicked, but think about this: even through all that pain and discomfort you remained courageous, and continued to move out into the deep. When you go back and look at your goals and vision boards, you planned for the struggle. You knew that you would need to put in work – *real* work and so you have.

Stick to your plan. You got this! You have been building a winning strategy that includes vision, hope, perseverance, and faith to get the job done. Today, hold your head up, throw your shoulders back and keep praying. That door you're banging on is about to open.

Scripture of the day: Galatians 6:9
"And let us not grow weary while doing good, for in due season, we shall reap if we do not lose heart."

Day 89: I Think You Better Let It Go

"Close your eyes and imagine the best version of you possible. That's who you really are, let go of any part of you that doesn't believe that." – C. Assaad

You did it – you beat them again. Today, regroup, rebuild, and replenish!

Scripture of the day: Proverbs 16:20
"He who heeds the word wisely will find good and whoever trusts in the Lord, happy is he."

Day 90: "The Desired Effect"

"It's a terrible thing, I think in life to wait until you're ready. I have this feeling now that actually no one is ever ready to do anything. There is almost no such thing as ready. There is only now. And you may as well do it now. Generally speaking, now is as good as time as any." – Hugh Laurie

"If you got faults, defects, or shortcomings" like haters, backstabbers, or weapons formed against you - whatever part of your life it is, I want you to lay it on your Bible. Let the spirit flow through. Because of Jesus' life, death and resurrection, He can heal, redeem and remove all that ills you.

The desired effect is what you get if you believe.

Scripture of the day: Acts 16:31
"So they say, 'believe on the Lord Jesus Christ, and you will be saved, you and your household."

Day 91: Be Kind. Always.

"Everyone you meet is fighting a battle you know nothing about. Be kind. Always." – Unknown

Be kind today.

Scripture of the day: Psalm 34:19
"Many are the afflictions of the righteous, but the Lord delivers him out of them all."

Day 92: Shine Beautiful Woman

"Let them judge you. Let them misunderstand you. Let them gossip about you. Their opinions aren't your problem. You stay kind, committed to love, and free in your authenticity. No matter what they do or say, don't you dare doubt your worth or your beauty or your truth. Just keep shining like you do." – Scott Stabile

Women are like the sun. Everyone has an opinion of them, even from a distance. Men who have tried to love her always fail because they think they are the center of her universe. Others point and mumble under their breath about her beauty, strength, family, and accomplishments –because on their best day they wish they were you.

Keep killing them with kindness – they will never understand you. Just like the sun – bold, hot, and the center of the universe, keep doing you. Nothing in a man's life works without you. I am grateful for you no matter what you do. Everything since the dawn of time revolves around you and even on a cloudy day a whisper, touch or a smile from you makes my day.

Listen, sometimes it's hard being the center of the universe, but don't doubt your worth or value because everything starts and stops with you.

Scripture of the day: Romans 12:12
"Rejoicing in hope, patient in tribulation, continuing steadfastly in prayer."

Day 93: Open the Door

"Change is never easy. You fight to hold on. You fight to let go." – Mareez Reyes

Change is like a door; as long as you don't move, as long as you don't turn the knob and push the door open, you will never know what's on the other side.

This is your life something is knocking at the door of your life do yourself a favor open the door.

Scripture of the day: Philippians 3:14
"I press toward the goal for the prize of the upward call of God in Christ Jesus."

Day 94: Be Done with It

"Finish each day and be done with it. You have done what you could. Some blunders and some absurdities have no doubt crept in but forget them as soon as you can. Tomorrow is a new day and you shall begin it serenely and with too high a spirit to be encumbered with old nonsense." – Ralph Waldo Emerson

It's a new day and no doubt the sun is about to come up and you have already won. You woke up in your right mind, alive and breathing. You faced every challenge from the previous day – won some and lost some – but faced each challenge head on. Those of us who dare to walk through the tunnel into the arena know that yesterday's beating is to be forgotten and the lesson learned will live forever.

Tomorrow is a new day – you are not allowed to bring the trouble, blunders and despair that you paid full price for into that new day. Leave the old nonsense behind because this week is finished and you have won.

Scripture of the day: Ephesians 4:26
"Be angry and do no sin; do not let the sun go down on your wrath."

Day 95: Woke

"No one looks back on their life and remembers the nights they had plenty of sleep." – Unknown

Sleep is a luxury you cannot afford. The world has spun out of control because far too many of us fell asleep. You must wake up and rise to take control of this life.

We need you woke.

Scripture of the day: Psalm 57:7
"My heart is steadfast O' God, my heart is steadfast; I will sing and give praise."

Day 96: Step by Step

"God will open doors that no man can shut." – Joel Osteen

You know God is about to do something new and wonderful in your life. You can feel and see it coming. These days seem almost like a long stairwell that you climb each day. There have been torturous days that seem like every step you take your door seems to move further away. There have been days that it appears that no matter how many steps you have taken, you didn't move at all.

But here's the thing you have to keep in mind: God is opening the door. Begin each day as you began this year on your knees in worship, whether he opens the door on day 127, day 170, or day 250.

Scripture of the day: Colossians 4:2
"Continue earnestly in prayer being vigilant in it with thanksgiving."

Day 97: Quit? No.

"The temptation to quit will be greatest just before you are about to succeed." – Bob Parsons

You have worked so hard to achieve your purpose. You have "cried tears from your soul". You have found the strength to stand when you did not have any strength left. You have been told to quit and have resisted. There have been days you thought you would quit, but your heart would not let you.

Now, as you near your blessing – now as you get closer to the door God is about to open for you, the temptation to quit is overpowering. Here is the thing about quitting: the history of the world is littered with the names of those who quit. But they, like the invisible man, beckon the question: were they ever really here? Listen, every face you see has had to overcome the challenge to quit. I am here to remind you to not give up and never quit.

Keep fighting the battle because some evil will not die until you defeat it in Jesus name.

Hey, you have always been strong. You have always had the power. Now go take what's yours.

Scripture of the day: 1 John 4:4
"You are of God, little children, and have overcome them, because He who is in you is greater than he who is in the world."

Day 98: I Like Mine with Pineapple

"Never water yourself down just because someone can't handle you at 100 proof." – Unknown

The egg shells you walk on each day cannot continue to be the feelings of some fragile joker who never appreciated your value anyway. Listen, stop measuring your words and holding back. Stop playing small because of the fragility imposed upon you by somebody else's emotions.

Don't go out there spitting fire and being angry because being ugly is a choice and you were not born that way. The fact of the matter is you've always been too much to handle for those who tried to control you. Frankly, the people who cannot handle you as you are those aren't your people. Find the place that you belong and serve yourself up straight, no chaser!

Scripture of the day: 1 Peter 5:7
"Cast all your cares upon Him, for He cares for you."

Day 99: Ain't No If

If poem by Rudyard Kipling (an urbanized vernacularization)

"If you can trust yourself when all others doubt you,
All we got is us and you shouldn't listen to them anyway
If you can dream and not make your dreams your master
I own my dreams and they do what I say
If you can talk with crowds and keep your value
If a throat punch doesn't work, cut them with the knife you brought wit'cha
If you can meet with triumph and disaster and treat those two impostors just the same
Call them both out and beat them both
If you can trust yourself when all others doubt you
If you can stay calm in the middle of the storm
If you can dream and not give up in despair
If you can stand in the midst of the haters and not slap one
If you can hold on when there is nothing left in you but the will to go on
There is no "if" child, you are a winner.

Scripture of the day: Psalm 25:21
"Let integrity and uprightness preserve me, for I wait for you."

Day 100: Free

"Accept yourself, love yourself, and keep moving forward. If you want to fly, you have to give up what weighs you down." – Roy T. Bennett

The time has come for you to be weighed and measured. Secrets, cookies, lies, cakes, deceit, brown liquor, bad decisions, and being around the wrong people – it's time to let them go. Let's turn the page and pull back the veil. You were meant to fly, not to be stuck on the ground.

The countdown has begun... 5...4...3...2...1. You have lifted off from that stuck place and loving the wrong people. Be free. Do what you have to do.

Scripture of the day: Psalm 112:4
"Unto the upright there arises in the darkness, He is gracious and full of compassion and righteous."

Day 101: Saturday Morning

"You did not come this far to walk away without the victory!" – Unknown

Lay there and marinate in your goodness and discipline. Those who tempted you this week are confused by your calmness and serenity because they do not understand, nor will they ever, that you will never be broken.

Yeah, lay there and marinate in your goodness. Victory is near.

Scripture of the day: Psalm 25:2
"O' my God, I trust in you; let me not be ashamed; let not my enemies triumph over me."

Day 102: Listen to Your Heart

"'It is impossible,' said Pride. 'It's risky,' said Experience. 'It's pointless' said Reason. 'Do it,' said the Heart." – Unknown

No matter which direction you turn, there is a challenge. Up until now, I thought that each challenge came with an "if" statement. You know - "if" I do this thing, "this" could happen or "if" I do that this could happen. Do not lean on your own understanding or pride, experience, and reason. Instead, lay your head on the chest of Christ and listen to that beautiful heart that He gave you.

Scripture of the day: Psalm 16:9
"Therefore my heart is glad, and my glory rejoices; my flesh also will rest in hope."

Day 103: Remember, I Am...

"Can you remember who you were before the world told you who you should be?" – Danielle LaPorte

You are wonderfully made. But because life has banged you up, your settings are off. It is time for you to be reset back to the manufacturer's standards. There are three formal standards:

> 1. You are made in God's image, so there is never a day when you are not beautiful.
> 2. You are endowed with the breath of God himself; nothing you breathe on shall ever be the same.
> 3. You are the living personification of God himself.

Walk in your God given power with boldness, kindness, strength, and humility.

Now that you know who you are, go out and be amazing.

Be wonderful.

Be marvelous.

I am.

Scripture of the day: Proverbs 12:24a and 27b
"The hand of the diligent will rule... but diligence is man's precious possession."

Day 104: I Love the Woman You've Become

"The strength of a woman is not measured by the impact that all her hardships in life have had on her but the strength of a woman is measured by extent of her refusal to allow those hardships to dictate her and who she becomes." – C. Joywell C.

A woman can do what most cannot. Just look at her list:

- Bring forth life; surely the strength of a woman is forged through the life she has led.
- Makes good decisions, bad decisions, and not let either destroy her belief in herself as she still holds her head high.
- Her strength has been forged at the intersection of Love Lane and Tough Row, but that is not what makes her strong.

As an observer, what makes a woman strong is the battles she fought, the love she has given away, the trust that has been betrayed so often that she did what Jesus said: 70 times seven and if you count yesterday she is at 485.

The strength of a woman is built upon her courage to trust, her willingness to care, her ability to be kind, her faithful walk, and her refusal to allow her past to dictate who she is and who she becomes.

Scripture of the day: Jude 20
"But you, beloved, building yourselves up on your most holy faith praying in the Holy Spirit."

Day 105: Speak Fire into Your Life

"Everything you need is already inside of you. Don't wait for others to light your fire. You have your own matches." - Unknown

This world spends so much money, effort, and time telling you what you need; telling you if you "just do this, you can change your life". And for some of us, we are no better than Elmer J. Fudd hunting rascally rabbits. Simply put, we look in the wrong place. Looking for love – can't find it in him if you don't love you. Looking for fulfillment at work – can't find it there until you make it the job you want, not the job you have.

Listen, everything you need you already have. Let's start with what you may have forgotten:

1. When God made you, He breathed life into you.
2. Because of that, your mind is made by God.
3. Every positive thought you have is reinforced four times before you physically act.

I know you don't believe me, but I will prove it to you.

1st: You have your positive thought.
2nd: You speak that positive.
3rd: You hear that positive thought.
4th: You allow that thought to marinate in your soul.

So listen, it doesn't matter if nobody speaks life into you. God breathed his life into you. Speak fire into your own life. You have that power.

Scripture of the day: Philippians 4:13
"I can do all things through Christ who strengthens me."

Day 106: You Are Valuable. Be Fair to Yourself.

"If you expect the world to be fair with you because you are fair, you are fooling yourself. That's like expecting the lion not to eat you because you didn't eat him." – John Spence

Your sense of honor and dignity is what separates you from those who wish they were you. Continue to live with honor, integrity and dignity as you close this week in victory. Please remember this as you review your activities this week. Be fair to yourself in judgement of your interactions and assignments. The goal for next week is not to beat the competition, but to be better than you were the week before.

Scripture of the day: Ecclesiastes 9:10
"Whatever your hand finds to do, do it with your might; for there is no work or device or knowledge or wisdom in the grave where you are going."

Day 107: You Will Stand Before Kings

"No one is you and that's your power." – Dave Grohl

You are who you are becoming. All the places you have been, all the people you have seen, all the pretenders and jokers who have told you couldn't not do this or you will never be that have all gone away and will never comeback. Now that we know the limits of their power was just the noise of cowards, stand tall today and remember this: no one is you and that's your superpower,

Scripture of the day: Proverbs 22:29
"Do you see a man who excels in his work? He will stand before kings he will stand before unknown men."

Day 108: You Have to Listen to Your Heart.

"Be bold enough to use your voice, be brave enough to listen to your heart, and strong enough to live the life you've always imagined." – Unknown

You went through hell and kept on going. There is no need to drop the ball now.

Today you woke up and realized that the life you have lived was a dream.

Finally, you have to listen to your heart.

Scripture of the day: Proverbs 4:23
"Keep your heart with all diligence, for out of it spring the issues of life."

Day 109: Not a Sound

"Not all hustle is loud. Sometimes hustle is just you, all alone, grinding while no one hears a sound." – Unknown

You are the silence that your enemy fears.

Scripture of the day: Proverbs 23:7a
"For as he thinks his heart, so is he."

Day 110: Be Who You Were Meant to Be

"Don't ever be afraid to shine. Remember, the sun doesn't care if it blinds you." – Unknown

You are magnificent and there is no one like you in the entire world. Do not hide your skills from the world; there is no need for you to hold back because of the insecurity of others. No more playing small just to keep your friends. If you must play small to keep your little friends, it's time to go out and get some bigger friends, with bigger ambitions and larger minds.

You are meant to be more than you have allowed yourself to become at this point.

Scripture of the day: Romans 8:25
"But if we hope for what we do not see, we eagerly wait for it with perseverance."

Day 111: Queens Never Bow!

"A queen will always turn pain into power." – Unknown

The power in a woman's hands allows her to hold onto those things that exceed her grasp. The power of a woman's arms allows her to not only carry the burdens of her day, but her arms are so powerful that they contain the gentleness to swaddle a child and the power to hug the most rugged of men.

A woman's legs are so powerful that they allow her to climb the ladder of success and wade through hypocrisy of unequal pay. The power within a woman's mind is so daunting that her thoughts about "Pi" were so deep, a simple man could only respond, "I prefer apple."

A woman's heart is so powerful and strong because it has been left unfulfilled so many times that if it was not for her power, she would and could not love again.

So yes, "a queen will always turn her pain into power." Remember regardless the pain a queen may bend, but a queen will never bow.

Scripture of the day: Psalm 34:19
"Many are the afflictions of the righteous, but the Lord delivers him out of them all."

Day 112: Keep Your Mind on the Grind

"Stay busy. If you keep your grind right, it'll keep your mind right." - Unknown

Life is filled with many distractions. Distractions are not created to keep you from your work but created to keep you from your purpose. So, decide upon your purpose, joy, and your love and stay busy to achieve those goals because when your life is over, it will come to an end.

It is better to go to heaven knowing your purpose is complete, your joy has been real, and your Lord allowed you to find a rib that fits.

Scripture of the day: Isaiah 1:19
"If you are willing and obedient, you shall eat the good of the land."

Day 113: "You Can Dance Underwater and Not Get Wet"

"I asked God why are you taking me through the troubled waters? He replied, *'because your enemies can't swim.'"* – Unknown

Most days it seems as though we stand in the midst of troubled waters nearly drowning with our feet resting on the bottom of the abyss we call living, wading in the water never knowing what lies in the murky depths of our enemies' souls. You are never sure why you are always feelings as if you are about to drown, but alas, thanks be unto Jesus, now you understand how and why: *"You can dance underwater and not get wet."*

Keep in mind that your enemy pursues you and seeks your demise as long as you are on the path of purpose to your higher calling. So, my friend, continue going through the troubled waters that the Lord leads you through. Remember, the enemy can't swim because it cannot match your strokes.

It's a new day; rest upon the shore this day knowing that your days of battling the rapids of the troubled waters are coming to an end. The Lord will bless you.

Scripture of the day: Ephesians 5:20
"Giving thanks always for all things to God the Father in the name of our Lord Jesus Christ."

Day 114: Your Smile Matters

"The day will be what you make it, so rise, like the sun and burn." – William C. Hannan

Make having a smile on your face a priority today. You work so hard at chasing, competing and winning. Today, make smiling a priority and see just how easy it is to change someone's day.

Scripture of the day: Proverbs 15:30
"The light of the eyes rejoices the heart, and a good report makes the bones healthy."

Day 115: Go to Where You Are Supposed to Be

Are you where you are supposed to be?

I will be where I am at almost seems like a reasonable answer to the question, but I am not talking about being reasonable. As we plan our week, think about that question *are you where you're supposed to be?*

As my friend, Ed, would say, "are you fighting the right fight?" We have all been called to a higher purpose or calling but far too often we do not pursue it either out of fear or loathing. Your calling is not about you; it is about those who would be blessed by you being in the right place. Think about it this way – *"I will open the windows of heaven and pour you out a blessing that you would not have room enough to receive" - Malachi 3:10c.* Consider this: what happens if you don't stand under a window?

Go now, and get where you are supposed to be.

Scripture of the day: Philippians 4:19
"And my God shall supply all your need according to His riches in glory by Christ Jesus."

Day 116: Yes, You Are Great!

"What right do you have not to be great?" – Unknown

The time has come for you to embrace your greatness. You no longer have the time to hide behind the synonyms that allow for your comfort, strength, might, boss and power. The fact of the matter is you possess a natural ability and right to be better than all the others.

Stop being afraid of what people will think of you as your greatness emerges. Remember, they are not your people and you are not like them.

Now repeat after me: *I AM GREAT!*

Scripture of the day: Proverbs 13:19a
"A desire accomplished is sweet to the soul."

Day 117: Set the Foundation Appropriately

"A strong woman isn't afraid to tell it like it is. She knows her words are powerful and can be used to build people up or put people in their place." – Unknown

How will you use your power today?

Scripture of the day: Ephesians 6:8
"Knowing that whatever good anyone does he will receive the same from the Lord, whether he is a slave or free."

Day 118: 'X' Marks the Spot

"Happiness starts with you, not with your relationships, not with your job, not with your money, not with your circumstances, but with you." – Unknown

Every man and woman are on a treasure hunt – whether they are on a hunt for success, money, peace of mind, or love – we all know the hunt will end one day. We are all seeking the proverbial "X" that marks the spot. You can search the world over looking and trying to find the "X", not realizing that you've already found the "X". You've been standing on top of it.

I know, you saw that coming, right? But it is you and here is how I know: you have tried being everything he needs, but it didn't work out. You have done all she has asked for, and she still was not happy. You have met every metric at work, still underpaid and not happy. The result of not being happy is an extension of you helping to find everyone else's "X".

Today, place both hands firmly on your happiness, continue to help those who are in need, and know this – it's okay to be happy. You know where your "X" is now, so wipe the dirt and dust off of it and dance your happy dance.

Scripture of the day: Proverbs 3:13
"Happy is the man who finds wisdom and the man who gains understanding."

Day 119: You Cannot Be Stopped!

"Behind me is infinite power, before me is endless possibility, around me is boundless opportunity." – Unknown

Open your eyes to what is around you. We tend to close ourselves off because the things we want seem to be beyond our grasp, but they aren't. If we need to reach a thing high up on a shelf, we use a ladder. If a person is blind, they have a guide dog. Both the ladder and the guide dog help you get to where you need to be.

You are a juggernaut in motion and you cannot be stopped. Decide what you want to do for the next six months, make a list and let's get after it.

Start with finding your ladder and guide dog. Be open to the fact that there is more than one person or book that will fill those roles.

Boundless opportunity awaits you – are you ready? Good. Let's go!

Scripture of the day: Matthew 21:22
"And whatever things you ask in prayer, believing, you will receive."

Day 120: You Will Know Your Door

"If God shuts a door, stop banging on it! Trust that whatever is behind it is not meant for you." – Unknown

Hey, it's a new day! You are beginning to accept the changes that have been taking place in your life, which is good! It's time to stop visiting old places, old memories and people who mean you no good.

Those doors are closed for good. Begin to look at all the new doors on your path and you will know which one to open.

Scripture of the day: Psalm 118:8
"It is better to trust in the Lord than to put confidence in man."

Day 121: Hey, You Got This!

"I hope you know you are capable, brave, and magnificent even when it feels like you are not." – Unknown

As you lay there trying to figure out how to keep the day from beginning, remember these three words: Capable, Brave, and Magnificent.

You have the ability to endure pain and danger and your bravery is limitless. Your heart and soul are impressively elaborate and deep.

It's a new day and it is time to give the world what it's been waiting for. You are God's most magnificent, capable and brave soul.

Scripture of the day: Joshua 1:9
"Have I not commanded you? Be strong and of good courage; do not be afraid, nor dismayed, for the Lord your God is with you wherever you go."

Day 122: You Are a Giant

"Sometimes you have to get knocked down lower than you have ever been to stand back up taller than you ever were."
– Unknown

For you and I, it doesn't matter how many times you must get back up, we have to continue on the path towards our calling. You will appear as a giant to your enemy because what they do not understand is that each time they saw you get knocked down and buried beneath the soil, you got up bigger and stronger with each battle.

It's simple really – you are God's seed! When you plant a child of God in the ground, they will rise up like a giant, stronger and more capable of withstanding any storm and overcoming every obstacle.

Scripture of the day: Psalm 147: 3
"He heals the brokenhearted and binds up their wounds."

Day 123: A Woman Without Fear

"She is clothed with strength and dignity and she laughs without fear of the future." – Proverbs 31:25

It does not matter the state of the world, you will always find a strong woman holding it together, whether she is behind the scenes leading quietly and providing calm and tranquility or out front leading the charge when necessary with bravery and boldness. She is always composed and her presence projects the honor and respect that she is due, yet beneath her serious and composed manner, lays a simmering flame that will consume her enemies. If you threaten those under her care or what she loves, she will strike you down and plant you like a post in the ground. She does not fear the future – no, she runs into the future laughing, knowing that she has arrived and everything will be okay.

She comes to the future with all the power, glory and majesty given to her by God, so no, she does not fear any adversary because she is strength and dignity personified.

She is a woman without fear.

Scripture of the day: Luke 11:9
"So I say to you, ask and it will be given to you; seek and you will find; knock and it will be opened to you."

Day 124: Keep Your Spark

"Do not let your fire go out, spark by irreplaceable spark, in the hopeless swamps of the not quite, the not yet, the not at all. Do not let the hero in your soul perish in lonely frustration for the life you deserved. The world you desired can be won, it exists, it is real, it is possible, and it is yours."
– Ayn Rand

It can all be yours. Stop waiting and go get it. It's never too late.

Scripture of the day: Isaiah 41:10
"Fear not, for I am with you; be not dismayed, for
I am your God. I will strengthen you, Yes, I will help you, I
will uphold you with My righteous right hand."

Day 125: Growing Season!

"Always go with the choice that scares you the most because that's the one that is going to help you grow." – Caroline Myss

This is growing season, and despite the intention of people, no one can keep you from what you are to have.

Stay strong, stay positive, and stay faithful.

Scripture of the day: Proverbs 3:6
"In all your ways acknowledge Him and He shall direct your paths."

Day 126: Check on Your People

I want to share the following thought with you: *check on your people* – the quiet ones, the "I am alright" ones, the "I'm doing my thing" ones and the ones who seem-to-have-it-all going-on. You don't know what private hell or secret hate is doing to your people.

So, today when you ask how they are doing, stop, look your people in the eyes, and wait for an answer.

We are not all okay and that is the truth, so spend the time and check on your people. You aren't that busy, and if you are that busy, who is checking on you?

Scripture of the day: Romans 5:5
"Now hope does not disappoint because the love of God has been poured out in our hearts by the Holy Spirit who was given to us."

National Suicide Prevention Lifeline: *1-800-273-8255*

Day 127: You Better Believe It

"Your day is pretty much formed by how you spend your first hour. Check your thoughts, attitude, and heart." – Unknown

In your process of thinking, know this: you are great! As you cogitate your greatness, also know this: there is only one you, there will never be another you, and all pretenders will never get close to being you.

So, come on out here and put your greatness in action. Not everyone will understand your greatness but then again, you out grew them in the last millennium. Now, fix your attitude before you go out into the world and keep your head held high, shoulders back and smile a real smile.

There's a world out there waiting on you to lead it. You must own each room you enter; you don't have to be loud, but you should only speak to improve the silence. Leave your emotions at home with the nice version of yourself. You need to show up with some of your ratchet self this week – you know what I mean. We are not here to make friends. You are here to be intentionally and unabashedly great.

You got 55 more minutes to tighten up and pull it together because today we are only going in one direction. Some feelings are going to get hurt, but they will not be yours.

Scripture of the day: Mark 9:23
"Jesus said to him, 'If you can believe, all things are possible to him who believes.'"

Day 128: They Will Look for You

"Your value doesn't decrease based on someone's inability to see your worth." – Unknown

When you are in the wrong place and with the wrong people who do not value you, you are essentially hiding your greatness in plain sight. Unfortunately, they will not realize your value until you are gone.

Scripture of the day: Isaiah 55:12a
"For you shall go out with joy, and be led out with peace; The mountains and the hills shall break forth into singing before you, and all the trees of the field shall clap their hands."

Day 129: Be You -- That Is Good Enough

"Heavy is the crown and yet she wears it as if it were a feather. There is strength in her heart; determination in her eyes and the will to survive resides within her soul. She is you a warrior, a champion, a fighter, a queen." – R.H. Sin

You know who you are – now be who you were meant to become.

Scripture of the day: Psalm 27:1
"The Lord is my light and my salvation; whom shall I fear? The Lord is the strength of my life; of whom shall I be afraid?"

Day 130: Do What Needs to Be Done

"Rise up. Feel your power. Become the warrior. Know your worth. Be fierce. Dance the dance. Break down barriers. Know your boundaries. Shine your light. Respect your body. Accept yourself." – Unknown

The question is, do you know your worth? Not your perceived value – your perceived value is what society has tried to convince you of. Your worth is predicated on the fact that you remember who you are. God breathed life into you and because of that one breath, the vastness of the universe resides within you.

Yes, it's true! Life gets hard and sometimes we forget who we are. Shake it off and embrace your power, your fierceness, and dance your dance because since you have been gone, a lot has gone wrong. We need you back in the game to make life right.

Scripture of the day: 1 Corinthians 7:20
"Let each one remain in the same calling in which he was called."

Day 131: Take Your Hands Out of Your Pocket

"As you grow older, you will discover that you have two hands, one for helping yourself, and the other for helping others." – Audrey Hepburn

When you place your hands together to pray, you realize that you cannot help yourself without helping others. When you cup your hands and hold your palms upward, you realize that the cup your hands forms is meant to provide help, give hope, and pour out strength. This one thing I know is true – you have two hands. Put them together to help yourself and help others!

How you end the day depends on how you hold your hands. Will you hold them together to help yourself and others or will you stick your hands in your pocket. You have a choice to make, my friend.

Scripture of the day: James 5:9
"Do not grumble against one another, brethren, lest you be condemned, behold, the Judge is standing at the door."

Day 132: Prepare Only to Win

"Strong people aren't simply born. We are forged through the challenges of life. With each challenge, we grow mentally and emotionally. We move forward with our head held high and a strength that cannot be denied... We are warriors!" – Unknown

Today you need to rest, plan, and get ready.

There's a storm coming that we need to dissipate.

Scripture of the day: Isaiah 28:29
"This also comes from the Lord of hosts, who is wonderful in counsel and excellent in guidance."

Day 133: You Are a Warrior!

"You were born to win, but to be a winner, you must plan to win, prepare to win, and expect to win." – Zig Ziglar

You must create a detailed proposal for achieving your goals. You must have a ready mind, body, heart, and soul. You must visualize and anticipate you winning long before it happens.

Hey, you were born to be a winner. It's time to get used to winning.

Scripture of the day: Ecclesiastes 9:10a
"Whatever your hand finds to do, do it with your might."

Day 134: More Than Conquerors

"You can't win in life if you're losing your mind." – Tony Gaskins

Stop believing the lies people tell you about yourself. Now, these lies are different because you are stronger now than you were before. You see once you get stronger, the enemies words changed – they now use words like, *what makes you think... people your age.... women can't do that, etc.*

I know everybody doesn't talk to you like that but let this be a warning to you – watch the secret hate dressed up like a friend. You are strong, your will is powerful, and if you are not sure, ask God and watch what He will tell you.

Scripture of the day: Romans 8:37
"Yet, in all these things, we are more than conquerors through Him who loved us."

Day 135: Remain Strong

"The strongest actions for a woman is to love herself, be herself and shine amongst those who never believed she could." – Unknown

The indomitable will of women is unmatched. Her courage and will are unconquerable and her love and might have no equal. For a man to have a battle buddy is a good thing, but a man with a strong woman is invincible.

A strong woman – you know her when you see her – she lights up the room and she displays grace and mercy with a hint of fierceness. A strong woman is everything she needs to become "a homie, a lover, and a friend". She has a sweet soul and has begun to comprehend that she must love herself first and then she can let the rest of the world in.

A strong woman loves herself.

Scripture of the day: Psalm 119:134
"Redeem me from the oppression of man, that I may keep your precepts."

Day 136: Happy is the Goal

"Self-discipline is about controlling your desires and impulses while staying focused on what needs to get done."
– Adam Sicinski

You are the master of your life, period. Pay attention, understand your distractions and stay focused on your goals. Be sure of what your goals are and make sure being happy is one of them, however, don't scratch *every* itch.

Scripture of the day: Psalm 40:1
"I waited patiently for the Lord; And He inclined to me, and heard my cry."

Day 137: Composure is Key

"When you can't control what's happening, challenge yourself to control the way you respond to what's happening. That's where your power is!" – Unknown

It looks like you made it through the work week. The lesson from this week is *composure*. We must learn to compose ourselves in every situation – except love.

Why love? Because when you know, you know. When you find love that's real, it opens your mind to the possibilities of life. Your mind is where your power is. Open your mind and control your world. Your open mind is your super power.

Scripture of the day: 1 Corinthians 2:16
"For 'who has known the mind of the Lord that he may instruct Him?' But we have the mind of Christ."

Day 138: Answer The Call -- It's for You;

"God is going to send you places you don't feel qualified to go. God doesn't call the qualified, he qualifies the called!" – Unknown

Yeah, it's time to stop asking those questions and get your mind and your body right. Your day is near.

Scripture of the day: Colossians 4:2
"Continue earnestly in prayer, being vigilant in it with thanksgiving;"

Day 139: Focus Yourself

"Don't downgrade your dream to match your reality. Upgrade your faith to match your destiny." – DeVon Franklin

Do not let fatigue, people or problems cause you to settle for less than you deserve.

It's your dream and you have had it so long that nothing else is important to you.

So, right now, take a deep breath, focus on your dream and picture yourself having it all.

Scripture of the day: 1 Peter 5:7
"Casting all your care upon Him, for He cares for you."

Day 140: Win This Year.

Things we need to do, believe, or stop to win this year:

- We don't need their validation
- Stop comparing yourself to others
- Only you will control your actions
- You are no better than anyone else
- It's time to take a calculated risk
- Jesus is Lord
- Don't quit
- Move on
- Start early
- Read - knowledge is power

It doesn't matter what anyone else says or does. Remain focused on your higher calling and the Lord will bless you.

Scripture of the day: Lamentations 3:25
"The Lord is good to those who wait for Him, to the soul who seeks him."

Day 141: You Believed

"Every day, focus your energy and thoughts and what you want and take one small step towards it. Claim your dream has come true and believe you are worthy to have it." – Elle Sommer

Do not become distracted and stay mindful of your calling. Surely, there are a multitude of challenges, but most are meant to distract you. Think about who you were as a child and the passion you had for your future. The passion has not gone away; the obstacles have just become more complicated.

The funny thing is, the obstacles are the same – self-esteem, love, money, people – you just look at them through the jaundiced eyes of your adult self. Never stop looking at yourself through your happy childhood eyes. You knew you were the best in your world. You believed everybody loved you – starting with your reflection in the mirror.

Focus your energy and thoughts on moving forward, believing all that you have claimed is rightfully yours in Jesus name.

Scripture of the day: Romans 12:12
"Rejoicing in hope, patient in tribulation, continuing steadfastly in prayer."

Day 142: A Greater Call

"The greater your call, the greater the attack on your life. Know what's inside of you and fight for it!" – Tony Gaskins

The battle you are in right now is about more than just your soul – it's about the life, soul, and future of someone you may have or have not met yet. Simply put – your purpose here could be about how a conversation, a smile, or even just a nod of your head could be all it takes to change someone's life.

Surely, you are under attack and it is about more than just you. Do not allow the devil to cancel your assignment. You are strong, persistent and you must never quit. Yes, your call is great, but so are you.

The Lord has equipped you to win your battles, so dig deep and fight with all your might.

Scripture of the day: Hebrews 13:5
"Let your conduct be without covetousness; be content with such things as you have. For He Himself has said, 'I will never leave you nor forsake you.'"

Day 143: Strength and Courage

"Being deeply loved by someone gives you strength, while loving someone deeply gives you courage." – Lao Tzu

Strength and courage are not the same and neither is deeply loved and loving deeply, so the question is, do you have the strength and the courage to love and be loved deeply?

Today, be courageous enough to love yourself first.

Scripture of the day: 1 John 3:11
"For this is the message that you heard from the beginning, that we should love one another."

Day 144: Do What Might Have Been

"It is never too late to be what you might have been." –
George Eliot

Welcome to the next phase! In this time of your life, you will
make time for you. No, this is not the time to be selfish; this
is the time to explore. You have said no to a lot of things out
of fear and anxiety. Now, just open up a bit and do that one
thing you have always wanted to do.

Love like you have never loved before.

Scripture of the day: Psalm 90:17
*"And let the beauty of the Lord our God be upon us and
establish the work of our hands for us; yes, establish the
work of our hands."*

Day 145: Word Power

"Your words have creative power. Say it, believe it and you will see it." – Unknown

The power of words is enormous, and you must use that power with great care. The power of words will make people do extraordinary things; tell a child she is beautiful, and she will smile forever, tell a woman she is smart, and she will never cease to amaze you, and tell a man he is strong, and he will always stand tall.

Now, if you tell a child that she is ugly, she will hide herself away, tell a woman that you don't value her, and you will lose her, and tell a man that he's weak, and you lose a friend forever.

Choose your words well, for the power you have can lift someone to unimaginable heights or drown them in the deepest depths of despair.

Scripture of the day: Isaiah 26:3-4
"You will keep him in perfect peace, whose mind is stayed on You, because he trusts in You. Trust in the Lord forever, for in Yah, the Lord, is everlasting strength."

Day 146: She Winks

"A strong woman looks a challenge dead in the eye and gives it wink." – Gina Carey

I've yet to meet a woman who cannot achieve what she sets her mind to do.

Scripture of the day: Psalm 16:9
"Therefore my heart is glad and my glory rejoices, my flesh also will rest in hope."

Day 147: Room for Faith Only

"There isn't enough room in your mind for both worry and faith. You must decide which one will live there." – Unknown

The longest and hardest days are consumed by prayer, life and worry. Our hearts and minds believe in Christ and the salvation and redemption that He gives. However, our minds allow our lives to crowd out the goodness and the joy that our Savior brings.

Well, we lived a long time now and have seen a lot of things we can't un-see and have done a lot of things we can't undo, but there's no need to worry anymore and clutter your mind with pain of days gone by or of a future problem that may never arise. Cast out burdens, despair, pain, and worry upon the Lord. Your heart can't carry those burdens any longer.

There is only room for faith now.

Scripture of the day: Matthew 21:22
"And whatever things you ask in prayer, believing, you will receive."

Day 148: Follow Your Heart

"Sometimes you have to stop thinking so much and just go where your heart takes you." – Unknown

How many times have you talked yourself out of being happy or out of not taking a risk, then stood back and watched your imaginary self have all the fun? Well, it's getting late in the evening and the porch lights are beginning to come on for some of us.

Go ahead take a risk and seek happiness. No, they will not approve, but neither did they approve when you were unhappy. It's your life, so go live it!

Every day will not be great and that's okay.

There is no fun in perfection but there is joy in the living.

Scripture of the day: Psalm 62:5
"My soul, wait silently for God alone, for my expectation is from Him."

Day 149: Never Let Go!

"Love me like there's something in the air and it's killing us slowly, and the only way that we can both survive is if we don't let go of each other." – R. M. Drake

Find your love, hold on real tight, and never ever let go.

Scripture of the day: Ephesians 4:32
"And be kind to one another, tenderhearted, forgiving one another, even as God in Christ forgave you."

Day 150: Pressing, Pushing, and Praying – There Is No Other Way

"No matter the circumstance or situation, keep pressing, pushing and praying and God will keep refining you in the process in preparation for promotion to stand in His purpose." – Joaynn

It doesn't matter what has happened nor does it matter that they don't like you or that they pretend not to know your name. What does matter is that you must keep pressing forward, keep pushing past your distractions, and praying righteously to the Lord.

Yeah, you will change; you will be like gold and silver after the dross has been knocked away. So, with all the bumps and bruises that make you feel like you need to let go of your hopes and dreams, remember – you cannot nor will you quit because your promotion is coming. This victory is won on the practice field long before you get to the arena. Keep getting ready and learning your lessons, for when your promotion is revealed, you will humbly say:

I stand in the purpose of my high calling.

Scripture of the day: Proverbs 3:6
"In all your ways acknowledge Him and He shall direct your paths."

Day 151: It's Time to Go Bigger!

"It's time to go bigger than you ever thought possible. Do not try to hold back. No time for doubt. Step aside from the mind who doubts. Own your radiance!" – Amanda Marit

This is your time and your space – own it! There is no need to hold back any longer. The longer you hold yourself back, the longer you suffer in your mind. The mind plays tricks on you in your season of change – a mysterious illness, self-doubt creeps in and fear becomes evident, but don't be afraid.

Your dreams are wonderful and living your truth is freeing, so free yourself from the unrealistic expectations of the frivolous and grievous minions of your life.

This is your time and space. Own your life and dreams.

Scripture of the day: Romans 8:15
"For you did not receive the spirit of bondage again to fear, but you received the spirit of adoption by whom we cry out 'Abba, Father.'"

Day 152: She is Coming Out!

"A strong woman accepts both compliments and criticism graciously knowing that it takes both the sun and the rain for a flower to grow." – Unknown

Plow the soil and make ready for the harvest. She is coming out.

Scripture of the day: 3 John 2
"Beloved, I pray that you may prosper in all things and be in health, just as your soul prospers."

Day 153: "Bye Felicia!"

"Work for a cause, not applause. Live life to its fullest, not to impress. Don't strive to make your presence noticed, just make your absence felt." – Unknown

Understanding and proceeding in your purpose allows you to have unspeakable joy and living life fully makes you happy beyond belief. You stand out because of your kindness and the happiness that radiates from within, so when they, them, or your so-called "wannabe" friends show up with their negativity and lies, do not fret and do not cry. Just say "Bye Felicia!" and walk on by.

Scripture of the day: Proverbs 3:26
"For the Lord will be your confidence and will keep your foot from being caught."

Day 154: My God Given Names

"Start calling yourself healed, happy, whole, blessed, and prosperous. Stop talking to God about how big your mountains are, and start talking to your mountains about how big your God is!" – Joel Osteen

We have all been called out of our name before; we have even said and thought negative words about ourselves – but no more. We will no longer be somebody's maybe, I ain't sure, or "it's complicated".

Starting right now, I will speak and answer to my God given names. I am healed, happy, whole, blessed, and prosperous. God made you, God named you, and God empowered you – nothing can stand in your way if you believe.

Scripture of the day: Jeremiah 17:14
"Heal me, O Lord, and I shall be healed; Save me, and I shall be saved, For You are my praise."

Day 155: Rest Easy

"You will never reach your destination if you stop and throw stones at every dog that barks." – Winston Churchill

It's a new day; don't allow dogs of this past week to hound you. Relax and recuperate.

Scripture of the day: Matthew 11:28
"Come to Me, all you who labor and are heavy laden, and I will give you rest."

Day 156: It's More Than Math

"6+3=9, but so does 5+4. The way you do things isn't always the only way to do them. Respect other people's way of thinking." – Unknown

Open your mind to a new way of getting things done. Sure, the tried and true methods work, but we live in a wonderful time of innovation and self-expression. Look around your world and you just may see something new with your old eyes. You may hear someone new call your name.

Don't abandon the past, just take a look at your future with a new mind.

Scripture of the day: Romans 12:2
"And do not be conformed to this world, but be transformed by the renewing of your mind, that you may prove what is that good and acceptable and perfect will of God."

Day 157: Put Your Hands Together and Feel the Thunder and Lightening

"You carry both lightning and thunder in the space between your bones and your soul. Become the storm you are hiding from. A hurricane does not run from the rain." – Nikila Gill

Start the day knowing that the power you possess was given to you by God; in your left hand you hold the power of lightening and in your right, you hold thunder so magnificent that your whole world shakes at the wave of your hand.

There is no need to fear the sounds of the storms of your past. Let them dissipate in your memories like rain drying on an asphalt road. As you hold your hands high, lightening in your left hand and thunder swirling in your right hand, know that you are the bringer of the hurricane and with a clap of your mighty hands together in prayer, you now understand that you are the hurricane, and nothing can stand in your way.

Now, put your hands together and feel the power of your lightning and thunder, for you are the storm that God has made and there is nothing that can stand in your way.

Scripture of the day: Psalm 37:5
"Commit your way to the Lord, trust also in the Him and He shall bring it to pass."

Day 158: Let Your Light Shine

"The strongest actions for a woman is to love herself, be herself and shine amongst those who never believed she could." – Unknown

You have done what no one else could ever do – you have lived *your* life. You have lived through every smile, frown, the ups and the downs and you have become stronger and more resilient. You have blossomed into this sweet, deliberate rose whose thorns are celebrated for their stability and strength.

You are more than who and what you see yourself as. When we see you, we see confidence, depth, compassion, and radiance – a woman who knows who she is. So, go on girl – shine and light up the room. Those of us who care can't help but to watch and stare. Do not concern yourself with the uncaring, for they cannot see their own reflection.

Scripture of the day: Philippians 4:13
"I can do all things through Christ who strengthens me."

Day 159: Make a Memory

"Never forget a day in your life: good days give happiness, bad days give experience, worst days give lessons, and best days give memories." – Unknown

It's time to do what you have to do. and cast your burden on the Lord and leave it there this time. Yeah, I know you've been carrying that "thing" around so long it was starting to feel like a friend – a friend that was sucking the life out of you while trying to kill you every day. Let it go!

It's time to start building on those good days – the days that make you laugh out loud and cause you to wake with excitement.

Enough of the bad days and 'I wish I never met you" days as well as those days that you are grateful for the Holy Spirit stepping in and keeping you from doing a 5 to 10 year bid in the state pen.

Be thankful for the lessons learned – no means no and DNA stands for "do not answer". Now it's time to make the kind of memories that make your toes curl up just with the thought of how good it was, the kinds of memories that make people ask why you are smiling, and the kind of memories that make you late to work.

It's your life and your time to live it. It's time to never forget another day in your life.

Scripture of the day: 3 John 2
"Beloved, I pray that you may prosper in all things and be in health, just as your soul prospers."

Day 160: Don't Let Your Soul's Fire Go Out

"Be fearless in pursuit of what sets your soul on fire." – Jennifer Lee

This one thing about you is true whether you choose to believe it or not – you are fearless because as each day dawns, you prepare yourself to go into the day to do what needs to be done with boldness and courage to defeat depression. You must openly display an indomitable will in the midst of your frenemies, and you must gallantly stride through the pit of vipers who silently seek your demise.

You consistently step across the threshold on even the most difficult days to confront disillusion, angst, temptation, pain, and the adversary who openly roams around seeking your destruction, but there you are standing erect, shoulders broad, head held high, and fire burning with such intensity that those who love you are warmed by your touch, while the flesh of those who mean you no good drown in the embrace of their wishy-washy handshake.

This is your time, and don't let your fire go out. Continue your pursuit of joy, happiness, and peace as you carry the torch of grace and mercy. Let your soul's fire burn and let no man or woman extinguish your soul fire. You are fearless.

Scripture of the day: Colossians 1:10
"That you may walk worthy of the Lord, fully pleasing Him, being fruitful in every good work and increasing in the knowledge of God."

Day 161: Honor God in Our Purpose

"You have this one life. How do you wanna spend it? Apologizing? Regretting? Questioning? Hating you? Dieting? Running after people who don't see you?
Be brave. Believe in yourself. Do what feels good. Take risks." – Unknown

You have this one life so make yourself proud. It's a new day.

Scripture of the day: Isaiah 12:3
"Therefore with joy you will draw water from the wells of salvation."

Day 162: Your Mind Is Vast, Powerful, and Deep

"Life is going to get out of hand sometimes, so get up and get yourself together. You're either an ocean or a puddle. Don't be a puddle. People walk through puddles like they're nothing. Oceans destroy cities. Be an ocean." – Unknown

This is going to be a good day. Clarity will be the hallmark for this day. Remember to stay focused on your purpose. Temptation is lurking around every corner, but you are a vast, powerful, and deep ocean.

Scripture of the day: 1 John 3:18
"My little children, let us not love in word or in tongue, but in deed and in truth."

Day 163: Braver, Smarter, Stronger and Loved

"Always remember you are braver than you believe, stronger than you feel, smarter than you think, and loved more than you know." – Unknown

Charge into this day knowing you are braver, stronger, smarter, and loved. It does not matter what anyone else says. So, repeat after me: *I am braver, I am stronger, I am smarter, and I am loved by me. It doesn't matter what the world thinks I am or who they say I am. God is I am and I am is within me.*

Scripture of the day: 2 Chronicles 9:7
"Happy are your men and happy are these your servants, who stand continually before you and hear your wisdom!"

Day 164: It's Time to Shine

"A woman who walks in purpose doesn't have to chase people or opportunities. Her light causes people and opportunities to pursue her." – Unknown

The way you stand says purpose, the way you sit says regal and the way you move makes grown men want to look away but they cannot. There is no need to chase after him, them, or "it".

Stop hiding your inner light and allow your light to shine. All the things you have been searching for have been searching for you.

You are beautiful and smart, so it's time to do your thing.

Scripture of the day: Jude 20
"But you, beloved, building yourselves up on your most holy faith, praying in the Holy Spirit"

Day 165: Take the Step

"The best feeling in the world is finally knowing you took a step in the right direction; a step towards the future where everything you never thought possible is possible." – from Unknown

One foot in front of the other seems simple enough, but it's not. There comes a time when you have to grab yourself by the collar and throw yourself off the mountain. At your back are broken promises, lies and liars, and sleepless nights, and one step is all it takes to know your possibilities.

Scripture of the day: Psalm 100:4
"Enter into His gates with thanksgiving and into His courts with praise. Be thankful to Him, and bless his name."

Day 166: Kick the Door Open!

"I am here. I have the courage to believe that matters. I have the strength to make a difference... to *be* different. Even with an empty hand, I have the means to give. I am free to become... to fail... to learn. I have the advantage of hope. I have the opportunity to love... to be loved. I have the wisdom to know it is all a gift. When I make my decision on how I am going to live this day, and it is a decision, I joyfully, responsibly, gratefully, face the world and say, "I am here." – Jodi Hills

You are in charge of this day.

Scripture of the day: John 16:33
"These things I have spoken to you, that in Me you may have peace. In the world you will have tribulation; but be of good cheer, I have overcome the world."

Day 167: Make Your Paths Clean for the Truth

"A new thing is coming. Don't rebuild the past. Stop trying to fix everything to be as it was before. A new thing is rising; forget the former things and make closer paths for the new."
– Unknown

It's a new day; you've done well during the past week. Let's set our minds on the future and what God has for us.

Scripture of the day: 2 Timothy 4:17
"But the Lord stood with me and strengthened me, so that the message might be preached fully through me, and that all the Gentiles might hear. Also I was delivered out of the mouth of the lion."

Day 168: Don't Stop Now!

"Forgive yourself for not knowing what you didn't know until you lived through it. Honor your path and trust your journey. Learn. Grow. Evolve. Become." – Creig Crippen

You are where you are supposed to be so don't stop now.

Scripture of the day: Romans 8:14
"For as many are led by the Spirit of God, these are the sons of God."

Day 169: Burn the Box

"Hard times are often blessings in disguise. Let go and let life strengthen you. No matter how much it hurts, hold your head up and keep going. This is an important lesson to remember when you're having a rough day, a bad month, or a crappy year. Truth be told, sometimes the hardest lessons to learn are the ones your spirit needs most. Your past was never a mistake if you learned from it. So take all the crazy experiences and lessons and place them in a box labeled 'thank you.'" – Unknown

It may not seem like it most days, but yes, you are growing. We get bogged down by the illusion of other people's blind eyes. Stop worrying about how you appear to them; they never liked you anyway, so no matter what you do and where you go, you will never be smart enough, good enough or loving enough.

So, take the comments, little digs, rolled eyes and put them in the "thank you" box and set the box on fire.

Scripture of the day: 2 Thessalonians 3:3
"But the Lord is faithful, who will establish you and guard you from the evil one."

Day 170: Love Her Fire

"Does she scare you a little? Good. She should make you fear her love, so that when she lets you be a part of it, you won't take it lightly. She should remind you of the power that beauty brings, that storms reside in her veins, and that she still wants you in the middle of it all. Do not take this soul for granted, for she is fierce, and she can take you places that you never thought you could go; but she is still loving in the midst of it all, like the calm rain after a storm, she can bring life. Learn her, and cherish her, respect her, and love her; for she is so much more than a pretty face, she is a soul on fire." – T.B. LaBerge

A woman knows she is capable of so much more. Love her, learn her and cherish her fire that burns bold and bright.

Scripture of the day: Ephesians 2:10
"For we are His workmanship, created in Christ Jesus for good works, which God prepared beforehand that we should walk in them."

Day 171: The World is Better Because of You!

"In a world full of fear, be courageous. In a world full of lies, be honest. In a world where few care, be compassionate. In a world full of phonies, be yourself. Because the world sees you. The world hopes for you. The world is inspired by you. The world can be better because of you." – Doe Zantamata

You have no reason to fear your future. Just in case you need proof, consider this: you have lived through every day of your life. The heartache, heartbreaks, disappointment, and betrayals did not get you and there is nothing in your future that can stand in your way.

Listen, we are watching and cheering for you to win this game of life. You inspire people you don't even know with your ability to get up and go regardless of the conditions. The world has been made so much better because of you.

Scripture of the day: 2 Kings 6:16
"So he answered, 'Do not fear, for those who are with us are more than those who are with them.'"

Day 172: You Got What You Need

"Don't spoil what you have by desiring what you have not; but remember that what you now have was once among the things you only hoped for." – Epicurus

You have what you need to make today a good day. Love and enjoy yourself and smile and make somebody's day.

Scripture of the day: Psalm 16:9
"Therefore my heart is glad, and my glory rejoices; my flesh also will rest in hope."

Day 173: The Power Is Within You

"Within you beats a heart of a warrior capable of fierce battle. The same warrior prays that battle never comes. Within you are eyes that have seen too much, eyes that see too deeply, but eyes that your heart will not shut.

Within you burns a desire and a perseverance that does not allow you to quit. Within you is a mind that has blossomed into a masterful tool – a mind that is open, a mind that cherishes the men and women who have shared their brilliance with you.

Within you is a place that launches your passion, your laughter, your brilliance, your courage, and your boldness.

Within you is the same power that raised Christ from the dead!" – Unknown

Scripture of the day: Romans 8:11
"But if the Spirit of Him who raised Jesus from the dead dwells in you, He who raised Christ from the dead will also give life to your mortal bodies through His Spirit who dwells in you."

Day 174: Listen to God's Plan for You

"I know God has a plan. I pray for direction, to follow it, patience to wait on it, and knowledge to know when it comes." – Unknown

You have known for quite some time that God has a plan for you, but now comes the interesting part: will you be strong enough to follow His direction and leading?

Developing the patience has been the easy part because you have spent your days hurrying up and waiting. Pray that your vision and mind will be clear that you know beyond a shadow of a doubt which door will be the right door to step through.

Scripture of the day: Proverbs 3:5-6
"Trust in the Lord with all your heart, and lean not on your own understanding; in all your ways acknowledge Him, and He shall direct your paths."

Day 175: You Can Handle Anything

"The women I love and the women I admire for their strength and grace did not get that way because things worked out. They got that way because things went wrong, and they handled it. They handled it a thousand different ways on a thousand different days, but they handled it. Those women are my heroes." – Elizabeth Gilbert

The untrained eyes of the disrespectful and frivolous have no idea what it means to be you. Your strength built from days of trudging through the emotional swamps of life and months of mimicking Sisyphus, pushing the rock up hell's hill.

An enviable grace allows you to juggle your hopes and dreams with one hand while steering down faith's path with the other all while trying to breathe. Magnificent women are able to handle anything a thousand different ways on a thousand different days.

Scripture of the day: Psalm 3:2-3
"Many are they who say of me, 'there is no help for him in God.' But You, O Lord, are a shield for me, my glory and the One who lifts up my head."

Day 176: Get Up, Get Dressed

"Believe in yourself and all that you are. Know that there is something inside you that is greater than any obstacle." – Christian Larson

Live your life and stop worrying what people think. Listen, we all have a dream about what our best life is – rich, happy and successful. You are a mountain-moving warrior and that makes you stronger than any man, woman, or obstacle that gets in your way.

Get on with making your dreams come true.

Scripture of the day: John 14:12
"Most assuredly, I say to you, he who believes in Me, the works that I do he will do also; and greater works than these he will do, because I go to My Father."

Day 177: Create Your Thing

"You job is to fulfill your heart's desire. Your job is to fulfill that part of you that is begging you and pleading with you to follow your dreams, to follow your heart, to create your thing." – Brendon Burchard

Good morning. Your assignment today, should you choose to accept it is not to listen to the doubters who try to tear you down, to take a calculated risk and follow your dreams no matter where they lead, and to follow your calling and create your thing.

Now, assemble your team of bona-fide mountain-moving, Jesus believing, cold-blooded cerebral assassins because this ain't the mission for your scary friends. This is a mission for the hammer swingers and rock throwers.

As always in the event you or any of the members of your team should be hindered, tempted, or captured in any way, know this – Jesus will not disavow knowing you. Rest assured that help is on the way and you will come out victorious.

Scripture of the day: Genesis 28:15
"Behold, I am with you and will keep you wherever you go, and will bring you back to this land; for I will not leave you until I have done what I have spoken to you."

Day 178: Find the Right Road

"Never look down to test the ground before taking your next step; only the person who keeps their eyes fixed on the far horizon will find the right road." – Dag Hammarskjold

There's no need to look down – you know the ground is there. You know where you are going, so no need to hesitate. The only thing that can happen on this road is that it begins to turn, but our goal is to focus on the horizon and this is the road that we will own.

Scripture of the day: Proverbs 12:24a & 27b
"The hand of the diligent will rule but diligence is man's precious possession."

Day 179: Keep Going

"Are you feeling a bit shaken, maybe stirred, maybe fearful and doubtful and completely utterly, wildly terrified? Good. Keep going." – Victoria Erickson

You are moving away from the old spaces that held you back but breaking free will not be easy. I know you've calculated the risk, and on some days the numbers just don't add up. The voice in your head that once encouraged you now mostly says *I don't know,* but *you* know – you know that there has never been a better time to change your life and to follow your dreams.

Sure, you could wait, but what would you be waiting on? So, shake it off – the fear, the doubt and the questions like *what if I don't make it?* Well, you never will if you don't move. This is your time and there is no one more capable of bringing change to your life.

You are the best! You are amazing! You are ready!

Scripture of the day: Ephesians 4:7
"But to each one of us grace was given according to the measure of Christ's gift."

Day 180: You Are My Hero

"And if I could tell you one thing, it would be this: you are never as broken as you think you are. Sure, you have a few scars and some painful memories, but then again, all heroes do." – Unknown

Stop spending so much time reflecting on how life used to be. The scars will heal and they will remain ever-present reminders of your great battles. The memories – ah, the sweet memories, are the teachers that linger on the outer edges of our minds far enough away not to cause pain or worry, but close enough to keep us from going down the wrong path.

So, get up, throw your hands up and draw the power from the Son. Your light will never be extinguished.

Scripture of the day: John 3:17
"For God did not send His Son into the world to condemn the world, but that the world through Him might be saved."

Day 181: Keep Slaying!

"She was free, she was strong, and she wasn't simple. She was intense and sometimes she barely slept. She always had something to say. She has flaws and that was okay. And when she was down, she got right back up. She is a beast in her own way, but one idea described her best: she was unstoppable and she took anything she wanted with a smile."
– R. M. Drake

The ferocity in a woman is only misunderstood by the weak men who want to tame her spirit. She is smart, but not a know it all. She possesses a deep and quiet brilliance, an intensity that runs white hot and as cold as gold, and a voice so piercing that the silence is improved.

The best diamonds have flaws; her flaws improve her value because she is pressure tested. She is a confident friend and lover and a beast to those who mess with her children or her kin. Beautiful, fine, and gorgeous would do if she were just a pretty face.

You, my dear, are unstoppable. Obstacles rise and problems may come, but you are a woman and an unstoppable storm, intense and strong.

Scripture of the day: James 1:3-4
"Knowing that the testing of your faith produces patience. But let patience have its perfect work, that you may be perfect and complete, lacking nothing."

Day 182: You Are Built to Fight & Win

"Maybe it's not supposed to be easy for you. Maybe you're one of the rare few who can handle tough times. Maybe it's going how it's going because you're built for it... Don't stress a thing. It's going to work out because you're not going to stop putting in work." – Rob Hills Sr.

The tough times you faced, the ugliness you have dealt with and the smallness of men and petty jealousy of women has caused you to throw up both your hands to God and yell *why me*?

Consider this: The ugliness, the smallness and tough times would have killed your brother, sister or friend. So, accept the fact that you are built for the grind and built to win. Grab your helmet and fasten your chinstrap because this fight is going to be good one.

Scripture of the day: Ecclesiastes 3:8
"A time to love, and a time to hate; a time of war, and a time of peace."

Day 183: Nearing the Other Side

"You shouldn't give up. Fight for yourself and who you are. You've got to go through the worst times in life to get the best." – Unknown

Never ever give up. You have been engaged in this fight for your life, sanity, and love and along the way, you have found out who you are – loyal, ferocious, and much stronger than even you believed. Going and growing through the world at times has not been easy, but worth every sleepless night.

You are nearing the other side. The best is yet to come, and you are now ready to enjoy it.

Scripture of the day: Psalm 37:4
"Delight yourself also in the Lord, and He shall give you the desires of your heart."

Day 184: Rock Steady!

"This morning, let go of everything you didn't do right, the negative things people said and focus on all you are becoming." – Unknown

Relax and decompress. Contrary to what the enemy and his minions masquerading as your friends are trying to convince you of, you are on the right path and heading to the right place.

Enjoy yourself today.

Scripture of the day: Isaiah 26:3
"You will keep him in perfect peace, whose mind is stayed on You, because he trusts You."

Day 185: To Him Be the Glory Both Now and Forever

"Make it your mission and magnify people's strengths, not to highlight their weaknesses." – Lorri Faye

You are to build people up, so tell them how strong they can be in the midst of growth. The challenge for the strong is to understand – understand that just because they have a capability does not mean everyone is capable.

Encourage and celebrate those whose skills are other than yours, as one day, your skill in another time and place may not be sufficient for the required task.

Scripture of the day: 2 Peter 3:18
"But grow in the grace and knowledge of our Lord and Savior Jesus Christ. To Him be the glory both now and forever. Amen."

Day 186: Achiever

"Never quit. If you stumble, get back up. What happened yesterday no longer matters. Today is another day, so get back on track and move closer to your dreams and goals. You can do it." – Unknown

The obstacle - the thing, it, him, her – inevitably will always appear. The thing for you to do is fight, not give up and never quit.

There are other routes to your goal, but quitting is not one.

The fact that you have chosen your goals and destination is proof that you have chosen the road less traveled. Do not believe for one moment that your goals are beyond your reach. Accept the fact that you are different and capable.

Know this now and forevermore, regardless of what or who shows up you will achieve your goals.

Scripture of the day: 1 Corinthians 2:16
"For 'who has known the mind of the Lord that he may instruct Him?' but we have the mind of Christ."

Day 187: One Calculated Risk Is All You Need

"There is a statute of limitations on starting over. Reinvent yourself every day. Be the woman who walks barefoot and listens to the blues. Today, wear your fiercest dress and speak your fiercest truths. Be a phoenix. Be ashes. Burn down. Resurrect. Let go of the idea that you must always be who you have always been." – Unknown

It's never too late to learn something new. Now is the time to ask and answer this question, *if I could change myself, what would I change?* Figure out the answer and make a change.

Now, don't go and turn into the evil version of yourself – I am talking real substantial change, change that makes you and your family better. Clearly, you have things you want to accomplish, places you want to go, and things you want to have, but from where you are now, you can't get there.

It's time to take a few calculated risks – change your hair style, write a book, start a podcast, smile and laugh – do something new for you every day.

You don't need anyone's permission. God loves you.

Scripture of the day: 1 John 5:15
"And if we know that He hears us, whatever we ask, we know that we have the petitions that we have asked of Him."

Day 188: And I Am

"You are amazing and strong and brave and wonderful. Remember that today." – from Unknown

There will come a point during this day when you will hear a familiar voice echoing in the distance of your mind – a voice you've heard before, reminding you of all things you are not.

Today, turn your face to the rising sun and the warm breeze and repeat this to yourself: *"I am who I say I am, and I am."*

Scripture of the day: Colossians 1:11
"Strengthened with all might, according to His glorious power, for all patience and longsuffering with joy;"

Day 189: Fight Preparation

"No matter what knocks you down in life, get back up and keep going. Never give up. Great blessings are a result of great perseverance." – Unknown

You have been a fighter all your life. You are unique and different and not because of your willingness to fight – no, you are unique and different because of your willingness to prepare.

Think about it this way – every experience you have had up until now has prepared you for this time in your life. David went down and got five smooth stones. We know he only needed one. The other four stones were not evidence of disbelief – they were evidence of his preparation. Remember, he was a shepherd and his job was to always be ready to protect those under his care.

Well David was no different from you. It makes no difference when, how, or why the enemy may appear – you must always be ready to fight. You've been on top of the world and had to fight and have been down so close to the bottom and had to fight your way back – today is no different. You must fight.

Your blessing is on the way – keep fighting.

Scripture of the day: 1 Corinthians 15:58
"Therefore, my beloved brethren, be steadfast, immovable, always abounding in the work of the Lord, knowing that your labor is not in vain in the Lord."

Day 190: Time to Get Sharp

"This is the beginning of anything you want." – Unknown

What do you want? Do you know? I mean do you *really* know? Some of us do, but most of us don't.

Today, put an index card in your pocket, think about your future and write down every idea you have about your future self. Write down where you'll live, who you will love – including yourself – how much money you will need, how you will make that money, and who can help you.

We need to learn how to win. We need to systematically learn how to create a strategy for ourselves that teaches and allows for us to build on our daily, weekly, and monthly experiences. These experiences will impact our social, emotional, financial, and political environments and will allow for us to grow, win, and achieve lasting success.

It can be done. This is the beginning of anything you want.

Scripture of the day: Proverbs 27:17
"As iron sharpens iron, so a man sharpens the countenance of his friend."

Day 191: My Mind is Made Up

"Attitude is everything; new day, new strength, new thoughts." – Unknown

On the other side of that door is everything you want. The question is, do you open the door? Now, if you open that door, you will have to fight, smile, and think differently than you ever have done before.

Before you touch the door handle, consider this: you can stay where you are, snug and secure and never be more than what you have become.

Well, it's decision time – open the door. You are a God blessed mountain mover with a new attitude, new day, and new strengths.

It's your time! It's time to win!

Scripture of the day: Psalm 118:24
"This is the day the Lord has made; we will rejoice and be glad in it."

Day 192: Lives Impacted by You

"Maybe the journey isn't so much about becoming anything. Maybe it's about everything that isn't really you, so you can be who you were meant to be in the first place." – Paul Coelho

Take a moment and think about all of the lives that would never be the same without you being part of their lives.

Think of all the people who don't care for you at all?

Now consider what your life could be if you focused on being the best you – people's opinions wouldn't matter.

The best version of you is a blessing to those whom you love. A curse to those who dislike you, as they understand that your life is not impacted by their smallness.

Scripture of the day: Galatians 6:9
"And let us not grow weary while doing good, for in due season we shall reap if we do not lose heart."

Day 193: Speak Life into Your Vision and Make It So

"A strong woman knows she has strength enough for the journey, but a woman of strength knows it is in the journey where she will become strong." – Luke Easter

You've come this far by faith, growing stronger each day while overcoming every obstacle, every bad day, every bad love, and every bad decision. You've built up an almost superhuman strength that has propelled you forward to this time in your life.

Well, here you are in the midst of the next phase, thinking, wondering, and trying to figure out what you will do with all this strength. You can do whatever you want – that's right – *whatever you want.*

It's time to embrace all that you have ever hoped to become.

Scripture of the day: Luke 21:15
"For I will give you a mouth and wisdom which all your adversaries will not be able to contradict or resist."

Day 194: Take Courage and Do It

"Friend, there's a greater you inside you or you would not be frustrated with where you are. It's never too late to become more!" – Lance Wallnau

What do you want? What do you really want?

Now is the time to decide.

Today, make your list of goals a priority. Take action on something for you today that will make your future better.

Use the following objectives to make your success path clearer: determine a strategy to complete each goal, select a completion date for each goal and visualize how achieving each goal will be celebrated.

Expect obstacles, as obstacles are mile markers of your daily achievements on the path to success.

Winning is a journey that most are not willing to embark on. Most never leave the departure gate for greatness as they wallow in the stories of the afraid and those who have lost their way. You, on the other hand, are different than most. You know the sun needs a leader as it comes over the horizon heading towards the future.

You are that leader.

Scripture of the day: Ezra 10:4
"Arise, for this matter is your responsibility. We also are with you. Be of good courage, and do it."

Day 195: I Swear I Got It

"The world doesn't need you to know everything. The world doesn't need you to be perfect. The world just needs you to show up and give your best. So, lead by example, share your experiences, and inspire others with your actions and never hold your gifts back." – Unknown

Today, I want you to imagine that every person you come in contact with knows that you can and are willing to help him or her become the best version of themselves.

Listen, you are marvelous and one of a kind, so share your gifts with the world; that's why you are here – to be a blessing.

Scripture of the day: Acts 2:28
"You have made known to me the ways of life; You will make me full of joy in Your presence."

Day 196: Strong Witness

"What if... everything you are going through is preparing you for what you asked for?" – Unknown

The fulfillment of your dreams will surely make you happy, but what if all that you've prayed, hoped for, and dreamt of was really about God preparing those around you for *their* blessing? The Lord knows that you will be humble, thankful and gracious but what if your moment of fulfillment is a blessing moment for your village?

You are a blessing through your presence and perseverance to so many people. All of your trials and tribulations could be about God getting His people ready for their miracle through your witness. So, never give up and remain diligent in prayer and faithfulness.

Scripture of the day: Nehemiah 8:10c
"Do not sorrow, for the joy of the Lord is your strength."

Day 197: Welcome to a Brand New Day

"The beginning is the most important part of the work." –
Plato

In the beginning, there was the word and the word was with
God. A is the first letter of the alphabet, zero is the first
number and here you are at your new beginning.

Have fun, learn, teach, and be happy.

Scripture of the day: Genesis 1:1
"In the beginning God created the heavens and the earth."

Day 198: I Was Born a Winner!

"Don't despise the small beginnings for the Lord rejoices to see the work begin." – Zechariah 4:10a *(NLT)*

We must begin each new journey not with an expectation of victory but for winning.

Victory is an expectation.

Winning however requires strategy and preparation in order to bring about positive results. You must plan your win by first knowing what it is you want, determine the objective and create a winning strategy.

Prepare physically and mentally to do battle regardless the location or the opponent.

Win first in your mind the terrain and the opponent will not matter.

Scripture of the day: Ephesians 6:10
"Finally, my brethren, be strong in the Lord and in the power of His might."

Day 199: Be Bold

"The doors will be opened to those who are bold enough to knock." – Tony Gaskins

So, what are you waiting for? Go ahead and knock. You are going to need to stretch yourself to get what you want.

Being bold is what is required of you to make YOU great, but also to make those around you great.

Scripture of the day: Hebrews 10:19
"Therefore, brethren, having boldness to enter the Holiest by the blood of Jesus..."

Day 200: Stay Focused

"Stay focused on your goals, your peace, and your happiness. Don't waste your time on anything that doesn't contribute to your growth." – Unknown

Now is not the time to become distracted; you have important work to do. Be wary of long-lost distractions raising their heads in this season. There is a reason for your past to be behind you.

Focus on your present task, not the circumstance. How you have come to this time and place is not important; what is important for your life is that you do what needs to be done for you.

Self-care is important, attention to detail requires you to focus, and encouraging others requires you to be strong. Focus, my friend – your time is near.

Scripture of the day: Psalm 19:14
"Let the words of my mouth, and the meditation of my heart, be acceptable in thy sight, O Lord, my strength, and my redeemer."

Day 201: Go Girl Change the Game

"She is a game changer. The kind of woman that redefines everything you thought you knew about amazing." – J. Iron Word

It's time to flip the switch, raise your standards and play at the level you are intended to be on. The world has been waiting for you, my sister. Time to shine like never before.

It's your time. It's *your* world.

Scripture of the day: Proverbs 31:25
"Strength and honor are her clothing; she shall rejoice in time to come."

Day 202: Stay Strong

"Small minds can't comprehend big spirits. To be great you have to be willing to be mocked, hated, and misunderstood. Stay Strong." – Unknown

By now, you know who your small-minded friends are. Their language usually starts with *why, you are too old*, or *we should wait*. You were not born with a spirit of fear – you were born with a spirit of greatness.

As you walk in your greatness, people will talk about you, hate you, and misunderstand your actions, but you have two duties: continue to pursue your greatness and stay strong. The strength will not come easy and some days will be more difficult than others. On the difficult days look to the Lord – He is there for you.

Scripture of the day: Psalm 46:1
"God is our refuge and strength, a very present help in trouble."

Day 203: Get Things Done

"Remember, today is the tomorrow you worried about yesterday." – Dale Carnegie

You have control over the things you worry about. We tend to worry about the things we don't control. Make a plan for your duties and priorities for the coming week and see to it that they get done.

It's a new day, so find a way to let your mellow show today.

Scripture of the day: 1 Peter 5:7
"Casting all your care upon Him, for He cares for you."

Day 204: One Foot in Front of the Other

"Sometimes the smallest step in the right direction ends up being the biggest step of your life. Tip toe if you must, but take that step." – Unknown

Put one foot in front of the other. As simple as it sounds, some days it's one of the most difficult tasks to undertake. The plans that you have are not simple and they require planning, however, they are just words on paper if you take no action.

Tip toe if you must, but take action.

Scripture of the day: 1 Timothy 4:15
"Meditate on these things; give yourself entirely to them, that your progress may be evident to all."

Day 205: Create the Right Direction

"You need to understand that life isn't what you are given; it is what you create, what you overcome, and what you achieve that makes life beautiful." – Unknown

You've never taken the easy way. Everything you have, you have worked for – even paid full price for some of those bad decisions, but yet and still you have overcome each of those new obstacles. Yes, you *will* overcome every obstacle that gets in your way. You *will* achieve your dreams.

Keep going; you are headed in the right direction.

Scripture of the day: Isaiah 26:3
"You will keep him in perfect peace, whose mind is stayed on You, because he trusts in You."

Day 206: Wake Up Your Future is Calling

"She has been feelings it for a while now – that sense of awakening. There is a gentle rage simmering inside her, and if is getting stronger by the day. She will hold it close to her. She won't let anyone take it away from her. It's her time – she will not only climb mountains, she will move them." – Lang Leav

It's like a fire burning in your bones; you know it's time to change. Time to move on – time to grow. Stop holding yourself back. Spread your wings and fly.

Scripture of the day: Philippians 1:6
"Being confident of this very thing, that He who has begun a good work in you will complete it until the day of Jesus Christ;"

Day 207: Dance Like Nobody Is Walking

"Do the things that interest you and do them with all your heart. Don't be concerned about whether people are watching you or criticizing you. The chances are that they aren't paying any attention to you." – Eleanor Roosevelt

"It's your thing… do what you want to do…"

You've heard that phrase so many times, and yet you haven't done your thing once. Well, it's time to dance in the rain like nobody's watching. Stop wasting time thinking about what they are going to say. Why care about the watchers and the "not paying attentioners"?

It's *your* thing – time to do it.

Scripture of the day: Hebrews 12:2
"Looking unto Jesus, the author and finisher of our faith, who for the joy that was set before Him endured the cross, despising the shame, and has sat down at the right hand of the throne of God."

Day 208: Help Someone -- Give Yourself Away

"On particularly rough days when I'm sure I can't possibly endure, I like to remind myself that my track record for getting through bad days so far is 100% - and that's pretty good." – Unknown

Wake up in the morning and say *Thank you Lord for another day to live a life of promises, love, joy, and kindness.* Give yourself away today and help someone in need.

Scripture of the day: Hebrews 6:10
"For God is not unjust to forget your work and labor of love which you have shown toward His name, in that you have ministered to the saints, and do minister."

Day 209: It's A New Season – Are You Ready?

"Write down things you want to improve. Write down things you won't tolerate from yourself. Write down things you never want to see in yourself again and go for it." – Joe Rogan

The season of maturity is upon us, not the season of change and not the season of getting older. We've come to the point where the things we use to do we will never do again.

We will be intentional about making our latter years the best years.

Scripture of the day: Romans 8:18
"For I consider that the sufferings of this present time are not worthy to be compared with the glory which shall be revealed in us."

Day 210: It's Time for You to Fly

"*Come to the edge,* he said.
We're afraid, they said.
Come to the edge, he said.
They came, he pushed them, and they flew." – Guillaume Apollinaire

Of all the people in the world, this is the absolute best time to be you. You have the power and absolute authority to do and be who you want.

Do not wait for anyone to push you – *push yourself.* Push yourself into the rooms that you belong. Push yourself to conquer the goals meant for you to accomplish.

It's time to take flight – your future is waiting.

Scripture of the day: 1 Thessalonians 2:12
"That you would walk worthy of God who calls you into His own kingdom and glory."

Day 211: Go Get It Done

"Don't wait for approval. Not everyone will understand your vision. You just need to believe in yourself, remain positive and go get it done." – Unknown

At this level, you are thoughtful, respectful, and full of grace. Your rash decisions are few, however, you still wait far too long for approval to move forward. We need for you to begin to embrace the following statement:

It is better to ask for forgiveness than to ask for permission.

It goes against every fiber of your being to be held back, blocked, and stymied by someone who is afraid of who you are becoming. You cannot help or love them as long as they continue to tie both your hands with their insecurity and fear.

So, do what needs to be done. Believe in your vision and surely and most importantly, believe in yourself.

Scripture of the day: John 14:12
"Most assuredly, I say to you, he who believes in Me, the works that I do he will do also; and greater works than these he will do, because I go to My Father."

Day 212: Ain't She Funky Now?

"And then all of a sudden, she changed. She came back a completely different person, with a new mindset, a new outlook, a new soul. The woman that once cared way too much about everyone and everything no longer cared at all."
– Unknown

You knew this day would come – you've had enough. It's not about blame or who did what to who.

You are now ready.

Scripture of the day: Ephesians 2:10
"For we are His workmanship, created in Christ Jesus for good works, which God prepared beforehand so that we would walk in them."

Day 213: Get Fit for the Master's Use

"There is no need to control and force things to happen. You are right where you are supposed to be. Start flowing. Stop forcing..." – Kylie Francis

You fit perfectly in your life. There may be a few people who are a little tight around the edges, but accept the fact that they are no better than you, that you have outgrown them, and that the places you must go and the things you must do will not allow for excess baggage. You can adjust them to fit, but remember a size nine forced into a size seven stops your circulation.

Scripture of the day: 2 Timothy 2:21
"Therefore is anyone cleanses himself from the latter, he will be a vessel for honor, sanctified and useful for the Master, prepared for every good work."

Day 214: Who Sent You? *I Am.*

"When you are evolving to a higher self, the road seems lonely, but you're simply shedding the energies that no longer match the frequency of your destiny." – Unknown

So, it's happening – you have begun to notice the small people around you, and no, I don't mean people who are short in stature. I am speaking of those whose minds cannot see you beyond the limits of their mind's eye. These are the folks who will never grasp the concept of the person you are becoming.

You thought that cold, lonely feeling you had was because they did not love you. Nah, that shiver that crept up your spine was a cold wind warning – warning you to stop growing and evolving. It was a warning that they will change if you stay the same. The realization that your speech and vision have changed does not allow you to be hoodwinked, bamboozled, or led astray by the promise of a liar. You are meant for a great and more meaningful life than the existence you assumed.

Remember this: it is not the cape that makes you super. You've been super all along – now go be who you are.

Scripture of the day: Exodus 3:14
"And God said to Moses, 'I AM WHO I AM.' And He said, 'Thus you shall say to the children of Israel, 'I AM has sent me to you.'"

Day 215: You've Done Well

"Some days are better; some days are worse. Look for the blessing instead of the curse. Be positive, stay strong, and get enough rest. You can't do it all, but you can do your best." – Doe Zantamata

You've done well; stay strong and be proud of yourself.

Scripture of the day: Colossians 1:11
"Strengthened with all might, according to His glorious power, for all patience and longsuffering with joy;"

Day 216: Your Direction in Clear – Lead the Way

"The great thing in this world is not so much where you stand, but in what direction you are going." – Oliver Wendell Holmes

When you look around, everybody is going somewhere and it's not your place to judge someone else's direction. It should, however, be your purpose to be clear about *your* direction.

So, the question is, where are you going? You know where you have been, every turn you've negotiated, every hill you climbed, and every rock you've ducked. You have gotten up each time you have been knocked down.

Well the time has come to set your direction for a positive and meaningful life that you will be proud to live.

Scripture of the day: Psalm 23:2 - 3
"He makes me to lie down in green pastures; He leads me beside the still waters. He restores my soul; He leads me in the paths of righteousness For His name's sake."

Day 217: It's About to Go Down!

"God will put you where he wants… even if no one thinks you deserve the position." – Unknown

Child of God, I hope you're ready? It's about to get realer. You have been casting your vision for so long and it's now coming into focus. You need to believe in yourself.

Your hard work and your faith will keep you on the path you are going.

Scripture of the day: Psalm 1:3
"He shall be like a tree planted by the rivers of water that brings forth its fruits in its season, whose leaf also shall not wither; and whatever He does shall prosper."

Day 218: Yes, You Are Different & That Is A Good Thing

"One morning she woke up different. Done with trying to figure out who was with her, or walking down the middle because they didn't have the guts to pick a side. She was done with anything that didn't bring her peace. She realized that opinions were a dime a dozen, validation was for parking, and loyalty wasn't a word, but a lifestyle. It was this day that her life changed. And not because of a man or a job but because she realized that her life is way too short to leave the key to her happiness in someone else's pocket." – Unknown

There is no longer a need for you to grow "claustrophobic trying to fit into someone else's small mind." Get out and create the world you want.

Now is your time.

Scripture of day: James 1:17
"Every good gift and every perfecting gift is from above, and comes down from the Father of lights, with whom there is no variation or shadow or turning."

Day 219: If You Believe You Can Do A Thing – The Thing Will Be Done

"The strongest factor for success is self-esteem; believing you can do it and believing you deserve the best." – Unknown

There is no one bad like you.

Scripture of the day: 1 Corinthians 15:57
"But thanks be to God, who gives us the victory through our Lord Jesus Christ."

Day 220: Create, Command & Work

"Create like a God, command like king, work like a slave."
– Constantin Brancusi

I want you to pause for a minute and think about things you want, places you want to go, and who you say you want to be. Now, make sure you want change, and if you do, you must attack your goals as if your life depends on it – because your life does.

Surely, you can have the life that you want but you must create it. Let no one or nothing stand in your way. You must own every room that you walk in, know every eye is on you, waiting for your next move, and know this above all else, you must work harder than you have ever worked in your life.

The fight you are getting in looks like this: you just walked up to Noah's Ark and realized you are the third monkey on the ramp. The problem is only two can go, so will you be the one to win the fight?

Scripture of the day: Romans 8:37
"Yet in all these things we are more than conquerors through Him who loved us."

Day 221: Dream Bigger Than What's in Front of You

"I have a habit of dreaming bigger than anything I can see right in front of me." – P.J. Morton

It's a new day and you are right; there is more to life than this and for far too long you have wanted so much more. You have what you have set out to get, but right now it's time to go get the things you left on the table.

This next list of goals is about satisfaction. No, we are not chasing past glory or reliving dreams of a day gone by. Cast you your sail into the wind of your mind. It's time to go where we never thought we could. It's time to find out if our reach can truly exceed our grasp.

Scripture of the day: 2 Chronicles 15:7
"But you, be strong and do not let your hands be weak, for your work shall be rewarded!"

Day 222: Playing Your Position

"Sometimes we have to experience the things we don't understand just so God can bring us to the place where He needs us to be. Never doubt the season He has you in." – Unknown

We are maturing and must stop asking, *why me?* You have made it to this point and it should no longer matter. You have the wisdom to call down the power from heaven to protect and deliver you. I assure you a few weird and unusual things will be crossing your path this season. Just stand ready and prepared regardless of what comes next.

This season is about playing your new position. Keep in mind all you have hoped for, cried all night for, and prayed day and night for is about to hit in Jesus name. So, put the doubt away, unroll your patience, and gather your excitement.

Your season is about to start.

Scripture of the day: Lamentations 3:25
"The Lord is good to those who wait for Him, to the soul who seeks Him."

Day 223: All The Power You Need Is Within You

"And if I could tell you one thing, it would be this: you are never as broken as you think you are. Sure, you have a few scars and some painful memories, but then again, all heroes do." – Unknown

Strap on your cape and remember this – the cape is an accessory and your true power comes from within. You were born with an indomitable will, a mind so sharp that feeble minds bleed when they hear you speak, and a love so deep that pretenders only see their own reflection. So, grasp on to these letters that spell the word *hero*; they will help you understand who you are, which is:

H: *Hard-working*
E: *Expansive*
R: *Rakish*
O: *Outstanding*

You have earned your place in this world. Now stand your ground and be all that God has created you to be.

Scripture of the day: Psalm 149:4
"For the Lord takes pleasure in His people; He will beautify the humble with salvation."

Day 224: Your Light Is On!

"I stopped waiting for the light at the end of the tunnel and instead, I ran down there and lit it myself." – Unknown

I am proud of you! You finally got tired of stumbling in the dark with that blindfold on. Every day it was *wait, be patient,* or *your time will come.* Every year it was *wait, be patient,* or *your time will come.* I am also glad that you got tired of waiting for your turn to come. You've known all along that there has been something at the end of the tunnel for you.

The fact that you ran down and turned the light on yourself has changed your world and some people's perceptions of who you are.

You now have freedom and a well-lit path.

Scripture of the day: Psalm 16:11
"You will show me the path in life; in Your presence is fullness of joy; at Your right hand are pleasures forever more."

Day 225: Giants Fear Your Power

"You may be up against a giant today, but don't focus on how big your giant is. Focus on how big your inner power is." – from Unknown

You've got the power! The giant will rise, but not out of nowhere. You've seen him before, but now you got to be ready because the giant remembers that you whipped him every time. This time, when the giant shows, he may look a little different, but it will be the same giant you have beaten each time. Don't be afraid and don't back down because this giant will fall.

You've got work to do.

Now, get to getting and change the world.

Scripture of the day: Ecclesiastes 9:10a
"Whatever your hand finds to do, do it with your might;"

Day 226: Stay The Course

"To embark on the journey towards your goals and dreams requires bravery. To remain on that path requires courage. The bridge that merges the two is commitment." – Steve Maraboli

Not a day has gone by in your entire life that did not require you to be brave. Some people call what you do being brave, but not you – you live your life knowing that there is no boogeyman and no monster under the bed. Your day requires that you face infirmities, reproaches, needs, persecutions and distresses to stand and fight for yourself against the enemy. Day in and day out, you muster the courage to keep going to keep fighting towards the goals you have set for yourself. You fight the brave fight, full of courage to prove to yourself that whatever you set your mind to, you will do.

Scripture of the day: Proverbs 1:5
"A wise man will hear and increase learning, and a man of understanding will attain wise counsel."

Day 227: Your Unique Impact

"You are so strong and so capable of so many wonderful things." – Unknown

Being you is not easy, but you should not ever want to be anyone else. The sheer magic that you bring to each encounter, whether someone is happy to see you or they wish they had never met you – your unique impact on people is singularly yours.

It's another day, so go bask in the strength that is you as others marvel at your ability to press on, be strong and show your mastery, depth and breadth, as you are capable of so many wonderful things.

Go be wonderful today.

Scripture of the day: Proverbs 16:20
"He who heeds the word wisely will find good, and whoever trusts in the Lord, happy is he."

Day 228: Today Another Fight

"There comes a point where it all becomes too much when we get too tired to fight anymore. Yeah, but today ain't that day." – Cristina Yang, from *Grey's Anatomy*

Today is the day we go out and beat the boots off our giants. Today, leave the quitting and whining to the quitters and the whiners because you've got work to do. Listen, making your dreams come true isn't easy; you didn't put in all this work to quit or come up short, so don't let being tired make a quitter out of you.

Today, is the day when you create a new standard. Start right and end right. Here's a reminder: Keep your head on a swivel; tempestuous giants are lurking nearby. Remember, the giants now disguise themselves, so be discerning.

Prepare yourself you got work to do.

Scripture of the day: 1 Peter 4:12-13
"Beloved, do not think it strange concerning the fiery trial which is to try you, as though some strange thing happened to you; but rejoice to the extent that you partake of Christ's sufferings, that when His glory is revealed, you may also be glad with exceeding joy."

Day 229: Burning Desire

"There is one quality which one must possess to win, and that's the definiteness of purpose, the knowledge of what one wants and a burning desire to possess it." – Napoleon Hill

You have trained your mind to do your work, trained your body to perform its daily duty under all conditions, and continue to train your soul to do God's will. You know the rewards that you pursue – your pay for a job well done, a metal for a tough battle fought, and to hear the Lord say at the end of your days, *"well done my good and faithful servant."*

The burning intensity within you – let it drive you to new heights. You will love the view from where you are going.

Scripture of the day: Job 36: 11
"If they obey and serve Him, they shall spend their days in prosperity, and their years in pleasures."

Day 230: Become Hard to Kill

"No man has the right to be an amateur in the matter of physical training. It is a shame for a man to grow old without seeing the beauty of which his body is capable." – Socrates

I pray that you never have to fight for your life, but if that day ever arises, you must be fit to remove all doubt that you will win. Train to be ready, train as a form of self-care, and train to remove all doubt that whether it be man or illness, what will die that day will not be you.

Scripture of the day: Luke 10:19
"Behold, I give you the authority to trample on serpents and scorpions, and over all the power of the enemy, and nothing shall by any means hurt you."

Day 231: It's Time to Grow

"If you know me based on who I was a year ago, you don't know me at all. My growth game is strong. Allow me to reintroduce myself." – Unknown

I am faithful.
I am loyal.
I am strong.
I am patient.
I am kind.
I am growing.

Scripture of the day: Philippians 2:13
For it is God who works in you both to will and to do for His good pleasure."

Day 232: Limitless Future

"When you develop yourself to the point where you believe in yourself so strongly that you know you can accomplish anything you put your mind to, your future will be unlimited." – Brian Tracy

Turn your brain on and go accomplish all that God has laid before you. There are no limits to your future if you believe.

Scripture of the day: Philippians 4:19
"And my God shall supply all your need according to His riches in glory by Christ Jesus."

Day 233: Strong Will

"The road might be long, the journey might be challenging and full of dangers. Take a rest, if you must, but never turn back. Your very next step can be your moment of triumph. Your very next battle can be your greatest victory. Keep walking warrior." – Unknown

You now must strengthen your will. When you find yourself fatigued and wanting to quit, you will continue on. Prepare your heart and body to defeat dangers seen and unseen. Resting is allowed, but turning back to the comfort zone is unacceptable. You must go to and be present in every moment, every day because you are in a fight. Every day you fight, you move closer to victory.

Scripture of the day: James 1:12
"Blessed is the man who endures temptation; for when he has been approved, he will receive the crown of life which the Lord has promised to those who love Him."

Day 234: All In

"Your talent determines what you can do. Your motivation determines how much you are willing to do. Your attitude determines how well you do it." – Lou Holtz

Your mind is a great gift from God Almighty himself. You are capable of building the longest bridge, capable of writing the sweetest sonnet, and capable of seeing into tomorrow and all that it will bring.

You are driven to greatness by the sheer desire to do and be the "you" within your dreams – a strong and mighty, barbarian with a heart. Now, the question is how bad do you want to be great and are you willing and able to persevere when everyone calls you crazy.

We are in territory that few have seen; most won't come out here where you are – not out of fear, but out of satisfaction. You do not have the luxury to be satisfied. You must push yourself harder, farther, and longer than ever before.

Welcome to the other side. Come on in and take your rightful place.

Scripture of the day: Hebrews 6:11
"And we desire that each one of you show the same diligence to the full assurance of hope until the end..."

Day 235: Day Break Is Coming

"A woman should be two things: who and what she wants."
– Coco Chanel

You have tried with all your might to be all things to all people only to find out that ungratefulness has no limits. *But we can't change that, so what do you want to do now?* You stand at this crossroad of who and what you want to be.

You know these two things to be true: "who" is only a choice that you alone must make and what you want to be is only limited to your ever expanding depth.

Understand this: everything you want has always been yours. Start today and be who you want to be.

Scripture of the day: Psalm 46:5
"God is in the midst of her, she shall not be moved; God shall help her, just at the break of dawn."

Day 236: Show Someone Kindness

"Too often we underestimate the power of a touch, a smile, a kind word, a listening ear, an honest compliment, or the smallest act of caring, all of which have the potential to turn a life around." – Leo Buscaglia

You don't know the private hell someone is living in; so don't underestimate your ability to bring good into someone's life.

Today, I beg you to pay attention to the people around you. You don't know the good that can come from a touch, a kind word, a listening ear, a compliment, or smile.

You just may save someone's life.

Scripture of the day: Philippians 2:4
"Let each of you look out not only for his own interests, but also for the interests of others."

Day 237: Being You Is Good Enough

"The greatest act of courage is to be and own all that you are without apology, without excuses, and without any masks to cover the mouth of who you truly are." – Unknown

Be proud of who you are. There are so many people who would like you better if you would do what they say, act how they desire, and speak when you are told.

God made you different, so stop trying to walk in someone else's shoes – they don't fit!

Be polite and be humble, but be who you are! Everyone else is already taken.

Scripture of the day: Psalm 121:1-2
"I will lift up my eyes to the hills—from whence comes my help? My help comes from the Lord, who made heaven and earth."

Day 238: Joy to The World

"Joy is a decision, a really brave one, about how you are going to respond to life." – Wess Stafford

You have made a lot of decisions in this life – who to love, where to live, what to do – and each time it was you having to do or care for someone else. Today, why don't you choose joy for yourself?

Scripture of the day: Proverbs 10:28a
"The hope of the righteous will be gladness..."

Day 239: Believe without Seeing

"Almost every successful person begins with two beliefs: the future can be better than the present, and I have the power to make it so." – David Brooks

How many days and how many nights has the thought, *the future can be better than the present* crossed your mind? The fact of the matter is the future *can* be better than the present, however, where most of us have a disconnection is that we don't start with the belief that we are already successful.

Think about it; our success is usually predicated on someone else's vision of success – a nice car, a big house, a successful career, but you and I must begin with the thought that we are already successful. You have overcome every bad day, bad love, and bad decision despite the challenges still rocking this life. Now more than ever, it's time to believe that you are great, wonderful, and successful in every way.

Scripture of the day: 1 Peter 1:7-9
"That the genuineness of your faith, being much more precious than gold that perishes, though it is tested by fire, may be found to praise, honor, and glory at the revelation of Jesus Christ, whom having not seen you love. Though now you do not see Him, yet believing, you rejoice with joy inexpressible and full of glory, receiving the end of your faith—the salvation of your souls."

Day 240: Embrace Your Greatness

"Keep away from people who try to belittle your ambitions. Small people always do that, but the really great people make you feel that you too, can become great." – Mark Twain

The question is not will you be great – that questions has been answered and the answer is *yes, you are great*! What must be determined now is how great do you want to become?

Spend some time seeking the really great people in your world. Now is the time to find someone to help guide you into your greatness. It's time to link up with the strong and great people of the world. Think outside of your box.

Don't wait – start today.

Scripture of the day: Proverbs 9:9
"Give instruction to a wise man, and he will be still wiser; Teach a just man, and he will increase in learning."

Day 241: She is Free and Fierce

"We need women who are so strong, they can be gentle, so educated, they can be humble, so fierce they can be compassionate, so passionate they can be rational, and so disciplined they can be free." - Kavita Ramdas

There are so many wonderful parts to who you are; for some, you are too much and for others you are a question mark wrapped in an enigma, but no one should ever be confused about who you are.

You are everything you need to be free – free to do, free explore, and free to live your life as you choose.

Scripture of the day: 2 Corinthians 3:17
"Now the Lord is the Spirit; and where the spirit of the Lord is, there is liberty."

Day 242: Joy Inside and Out

"Remind yourself everyday – I am in charge of my happiness. I will not let anything outside of myself control me. I am creating a life that feels good on the inside and it will turn into experiences that are good on the outside." – Unknown

It's great to celebrate yourself every now and then. There are so many things that come into our orbit every day that we do not control, but the one thing we must fight to have control over is our very own happiness.

Find the things that make you happy and do them, find the people who make you happy and go be with them, and continue to create a life that feels good on the inside. Your happiness will surely show up on the outside.

Scripture of the day: Ecclesiastes 9:7
"Go, eat your bread with joy, and drink your wine with a merry heart; for God has already accepted your works."

Day 243: Fight The Battle That Must Be Fought

"A warrior feeds their body well. They train their bodies and they work their bodies. Where their body lacks knowledge, they study. But above all, the warrior must believe. The warrior must believe in their strength of will, of purpose, of heart, and of soul." – David Gemmell

Feed your mind, body, and spirit well. Always be ready to fight and to win. It's your destiny.

Scripture of the day: Ephesians 2:10
"For we are His workmanship, created in Christ Jesus for good works, which God prepared beforehand that we should walk in them."

Day 244: Hold Your Head Up High

"Don't be discouraged. You're almost there. What God is giving you requires, focus, commitment and patience! Discouragement is the enemy's favorite tool to use against you. He knows there is greatness inside of you. Kick the devil in the teeth. Don't give up." – Unknown

Hold your head up high – God is getting you ready. Do not focus on your defeats; focus on preparing yourself for new blessings. Brush the discouragement off and chase the naysayers away. They know how great you are and there is nothing they can do about it.

Scripture of the day: Isaiah 41:13
"For I, the Lord your God, will hold your right hand, Saying to you, 'Fear not, I will help you.'"

Day 245: Dig in!

"Few people during their lifetime come anywhere near exhausting the resources dwelling within them. There are deep wells of strength that are never used." – Richard E. Byrd

Stop saving yourself for what you think may be the big meeting, deal, or job. Treat every encounter, meeting, and deal as if it is "the big one".

It is time to dig into your well of strength. Digging in does not mean by extraordinary circumstances – no, digging is about utilizing the skills you have. You have all you need, so believe in the strength that you have and drive hard to the finish.

Use the power God gave you.

Dig in!

Scripture of the day: Psalm 16:8
"I have set the Lord always before me; because He is at my right hand I shall not be moved."

Day 246: You Better Believe It

"The purpose of this glorious life is not simply to endure it, but to soar, stumble, and flourish as you learn to fall in love with your existence. We were born to live, not merely exist." – Becca Lee

Why are you here? *To be or not to be* is not the question. The question is why are you really here? Think about this for a moment. You, me, and everyone you know has been given a purpose, a dream, and a responsibility. Far too often most of us get our purpose confused with our dream and responsibility.

So yes, find your dream and go live it out loud! Tend to your responsibility with all diligence and integrity and accept your purpose. Stop running away, stop putting other things in the way, and go get done what God has told you to do.

Do it if you believe you can!

Scripture of the day: 1 Timothy 4:10
"For to this end we both labor and suffer reproach, because we trust in the living God, who is the Savior of all men, especially of those who believe."

Day 247: Why Not You?

"Today, I want you to ask yourself this one question: *why not you?* Why not you to do something for work that you love? Why not you to have a healthy body? Why not you to be, have, or do anything you have ever dreamed? The truth is that you are so deserving, so why not have it all?" – Jillian Michaels

Why not you?

There is no reason that it should not be you. Is there anyone in your circle who questions your pursuit of happiness? It is time for them to be placed in a new circle.

Scripture of the day: 2 Corinthians 9:8
"And God is able to make all grace abound toward you, that you, always having all sufficiency in all things, may have an abundance for every good work."

Day 248: No More Cloudy Days

"You'd never invite a thief into your house. So why would you allow thoughts steal your joy to make themselves at home in your mind?" – Unknown

It's interesting how the temptation of doubt lingers on the perimeter of one's mind. It doesn't have a burdening presence, but it's just off in the corner waiting to cast a cloud over your very good mood. In this season, doubt lingers about seeking to dash all your hard work, self-confidence, and joy. In our past, that would have been enough to destroy a good day, but not anymore.

No more cloudy days.

Scripture of the day: John 10:10
"The thief does not come except to steal, and to kill, and destroy. I have come that may have life, and that they may have it more abundantly."

Day 249: There Is Love All Around You

"Be careful with your words. Once they are said, they can only be forgiven, not forgotten." – Carl Sandburg

For every word left unspoken, there are probably five that should not have been spoken at all. Tell your people how much you care while you are with them. Apologizing when it's too late will never satiate your soul.

Tell someone you love them today.

Scripture of the day: James 1:19
"So then, my beloved brethren, let every man be swift to hear, slow to speak, slow to wrath;"

Day 250: Decide Not to Surrender

"Strength does not come from winning. Your struggles develop your strengths when you go through hardships and decide not to surrender. That is strength." – Arnold Schwarzenegger

I admire your will to keep fighting. Shake the hand of a fighter today. You know they are in a fight and it does not matter the opponent – just know that there are far too many of us fighting battles you know nothing about.

Never give up the fight.

Scripture of the day: 2 Thessalonians 3:3
"But the Lord is faithful, who will establish you and guard you from the evil one."

Day 251: Do You Hear What I Hear?

"No matter how many times an idea has been expressed or shared in the world, sometimes it takes that one person expressing it in their voice for it to actually get through and you are that person for somebody." – Marie Forleo

Never underestimate the impact your voice will have on someone. What you say, how you say it, and when you say it are all reasons for each of us to select our words wisely.

Scripture of the day: Matthew 19:25-26
"When His disciples heard it, they were greatly astonished, saying, 'Who then can be saved?' But Jesus looked at them and said to them, 'With men this is impossible, but with God all things are possible.'"

Day 252: Survival

"Your fight for survival starts right now. You don't want to be judged – you won't be. You think you're strong enough? You are! You're afraid? Don't be. You have all the weapons you need. Now fight." – from movie *Sucker Punch*

Before your feet hit the floor, the battle begins. The battle in your mind continues to rage on and the time has come to win this daily battle against complicit servitude and fear and loathing. There is no need to fear your ability to overcome and no need to search for the appropriate weapon.

You have all you need within you, but first you must accept that you are God blessed, heaven sent, and sanctified through salvation. Put away your doubt, stash your shame away, and erase all bad memories from your mind. Your purpose is to live, to serve, and to be an example of how good God is.

Now, pick yourself up, dust off your clothes, adjust your attitude, and go fight!

Scripture of the day: 1 John 5:4
"For whatever is born of God overcomes the world. And this is the victory that has overcome the world—our faith."

Day 253: Raise Your Head High

"To all the women who no longer believe in fairy tales or happy endings, you are the writer of this story. Chin up and straighten your crown. You are the queen of this kingdom and only you know how to rule it." – B. Devine

Today is the day you take charge of your life story. Tell the legend of a fierce, strong, and powerful queen and tell the world how great you rule.

You only have one life to live so go now and live it out loud.

Scripture of the day: Ephesians 3:12
"In whom we have boldness and access with confidence through faith in Him."

Day 254: Live Your Best Life

"You need to ignore what everyone else is doing and achieving – your life is about breaking your own limits and outgrowing yourself to live YOUR best life. You are not in competition with anyone else; plan to outdo your past, not other people." – Unknown

There are 7.53 billion people in the world and there is only one you! My friend, I have to tell you – that is good news. To live to see another day is a spectacular feat. With the rising of the sun today, you have the ability to be better than you were yesterday and to be smarter than you were the day before.

You are on the verge of living your best life. Now, there is only one thing you are going to have to do: don't look to your left or right to check out the competition – that is not where your threat will come from. No, your nemesis will be the face staring back at you from the mirror.

So take a good long look at that face and say out loud *I am better than I was and I am not defined by someone else's perception of me. Out of 7.5 billion people, there is only one me.*

Scripture of the day: Deuteronomy 20:4
"For the Lord your God is He who goes with you, to fight for you against your enemies, to save you."

Day 255: Faith or Fear Which Will You Choose

"Faith and fear have one thing in common: they both require you to believe in something you don't see. Which will you choose?" – Kylie Francis

There comes a time when your mind is closed shut and you begin to see the things that don't exist. You see doubt where it should not exist, you see provocation from the weak amongst you, and you become afraid of the utterances of the misguided and jealous, yet you shout *Save me Lord* as if he would not. Surely you can see fear on the face of the fearful.

There is a knowing glance that proceeds having to face an unknown threat or vague emotion or response, but faith is all around you each and every moment of the day. Your first breath, the opening of your eyes, to the knowing smile you share with your family. You can see faith in the hope that is brings.

So, you have a decision to make – faith or fear? The world's waiting on you, so what's it going to be?

Scripture of the day: Deuteronomy 31:6
"Be strong and courageous. Do not be afraid or terrified of them, for the Lord your God goes with you. He will never leave you nor forsake you."

Day 256: It's Time for You to Be the Hero

"Whatever you do, hold on to the hope! The tiniest thread will twist into an unbreakable cord. Let hope anchor you in the possibility that this is not the end of your story. Write your tomorrow!" – Unknown

A child will reach out his hand, not in the hope that a hand will be there to hold on to but *knowing* that your hand will be there. Well, child of God, in your case, Jesus is the 6one full of hope. He hopes that you know that when you reach out your hand, his hand will be there for you.

The Lord of salvation keeps your soul anchored. It is the hope of life that should fill you with the unfathomable idea this is your day, your month, your year, and your life. Let hope anchor you in the idea that this part of your life gets to be better than ever before. So, today begin to write the story of your tomorrow.

Scripture of the day: 1 Peter 5:10
"But may the God of all grace, who called us to His eternal glory by Christ Jesus, after you have suffered a while, perfect, establish, strengthen, and settle you."

Day 257: No Gilded Cage

"And the day came when the risk to remain tight in a bud was more painful than the risk it took to blossom." – Anais Nin

A couple of things could happen when you put a seed in the ground: if you pack the ground too tight, it makes it difficult for the seed to break through or sometimes the soil is just bad, and nothing can grow, not even weeds.

So, you've come to the point that no matter the direction you turn, it's just tight. Your breathing is tight, your creativity is shrouded, and your options seem few as long as you stay where you are.

It's time to break free of that cage. Don't allow yourself to suffocate in a world full of air. Break free and loose yourself.

Scripture of the day: Galatians 5:1
"Stand fast therefore in the liberty by which Christ has made us free, and do not be entangled again with a yoke of bondage."

Day 258: Who Are You Talking to?

"There are some people who could hear you speak a thousand words and still not understand you. And there are others who will understand without you even speaking a word." – Yasmin Mogahed

Who are you talking to and why? Who are you listening to and why? If life and death are in the power of tongue, then know this: there are those who could not heed a warning solely because it came from you. Therefore, be very careful with the words you speak. Although some may not understand a word you say, beware, as they will read more into the words you leave unspoken. That is the duality of the spoken word – people hear what they want to hear.

Your words have power, so use your power wisely, as someone's life, death, and freedom may rest upon the utterance of a bitter man.

Scripture of the day: Romans 10:9
"That if you confess with your mouth the Lord Jesus and believe in your heart that God has raised Him from the dead, you will be saved."

Day 259: Value You!

"Count your blessings. Once you realize how valuable you are and how much you have going for you, the smiles will return, the sun will breakout, the music will play, and you will finally be able to move forward into the life God intended for you with grace, strength, courage, and confidence." – Og Mandino

Stop for a moment and think about your true friends – consider them your first blessing. Now count the days of the week – that's seven. When you add in your salvation, you get nine. Those are just the one's you can count on both hands. Your value can be measured by the true and loyal friends you have, the seven days of the week that you get a chance to start reclaiming your life, and your soul's salvation.

You have so much to be happy about and to live for. So, throw back your shoulders and hold your head high. It's time to step into your groove. Come out here and bask in your grace, walk strong, and display your courage as you fight off your foes.

Scripture of the day: Job 8:7
"Though your beginning was small, yet your latter end would increase abundantly."

Day 260: Stay On Your Path

"Do not give up, even when others do not understand. Even when you feel alone with your dreams. Even when your vision gets a little blurred. Your steps are ordered and you are destined for greatness. You are stronger than your mind can conceive. Everything you need lies within you." – Lakesha Womack

You have driven so far past the point of no return. There are those who have stopped believing in you, but no matter – they *never* thought you could be great. You are pursuing your dreams, not the fantasies of someone else's small mind. Surely your vision gets blurry some days from the sweat and tears, but as hard as you work, you can't tell the sweat from the tears because they both taste salty in the heat of making your dreams come true.

There is no way for you to fail. God has placed you on your path and you will not be moved. Do not look for the tools, power, or strength; everything you need to be great is within you.

Scripture of the day: Psalm 55:22
"Cast you burden on the Lord, and He will sustain you; He shall never permit the righteous to be moved."

Day 261: Forward into Life

"Do not fast forward into something you're not ready for or allow yourself to shrink back into what's comfortable. Growth lives in the uneasiness and the in-between. You are in a season of becoming." – Unknown

This is your time. There has never been a time like this for you, so there is no need to rush. It is all beginning to come together. You cannot turn back – don't even look back because there is nothing there for you. It's good to be nervous; you are going into places you have never been before.

This is not a season of fear – this is your season of becoming.

Scripture of the day: Isaiah 43:19
"Behold, I will do a new thing, now it shall spring forth; Shall you not know it? I will even make a road in the wilderness and rivers in the desert."

Day 262: Intentional About You!

"Live with intention.
Walk to the edge.
Listen hard.
Practice wellness.
Play with abandon.
Laugh.
Choose with no regret.
Continue to learn.
Appreciate your friends.
Do what you love.
Love as if this is all there is."
– Mary Anne Rodmacher

Stop, close your eyes, and listen really hard. Listen for the passion, the pain, and the depth. If you are there just to hear, you will miss it. Walk to the edge of your despair and step over into intentional living. The harder you play, the more well you become. Come into the arena and learn to fight for your life. Every battle fought will not be a battle of wits. It's best to know how to beat the boots of a foe.

Learn to laugh at those things that are funny, but never laugh at people and their misfortune; that behavior makes you small and you are not meant to be small.

Love as if your life depended on it, because it does.

Scripture of the day: Isaiah 12:2
"Behold, God is my salvation, I will trust and not be afraid; 'For Yah, the Lord, is my strength and song; He also has become my salvation.'"

Day 263: Revived Daily

"With the new day comes new strength and new thoughts."
– Eleanor Roosevelt

Every new day should bring with it the knowledge that you were strong enough to withstand the previous day and powerful enough to endure the night that followed. The morning brings rejuvenation of your body and mind. Your mind is revived, renewed, and refilled with ideas.

Scripture of the day: Psalm 51:12
"Restore to me the joy of your salvation and uphold me by Your generous Spirit."

Day 264: Storms Equal Growth

"When you come out of the storm, you won't be the same person that walked in. That's what the storm is all about." – Haruki Murakami

Growth does not flourish in the quiet. No, growth flourishes in the midst of the chaos, the madness, and the noise. Your growth hinges upon your ability to withstand the struggle and the temptation.

Surely most would quit when the wind blows a bit too hard, but not you. You have finally begun to understand that the storm did not come to destroy you – it was brought about to make you better, stronger, and smarter.

The storm is almost over, and you are looking stronger already.

Scripture of the day: Proverbs 10:25
"When the whirlwind passes by, the wicked is no more, but the righteous has an everlasting foundation."

Day 265: Trust for Real

"You don't always need a plan. Sometimes you just need to breathe, trust, let go, and see what happens." – Mandy Hale

We tend to over plan to the point that life can become so over regulated that we are afraid to stop. Be clear, I am not talking about discipline or habits. This is about freedom – freedom to relax, freedom to breathe, to take in what life is offering you or better yet, what you have to offer life. *You have so much to offer in life.*

Trust in the Lord for real this time. No more one foot in or one foot out. No more rabbit's foot, four leaf clovers, or throwing salt over your shoulder. Let go of the disbelief.

Scripture of the day: Psalm 9:10
"And those who know Your name will put their trust in You; for You, Lord, have not forsaken those who seek You."

Day 266: Thank You

"If the only prayer you ever say in your entire life is thank you, it will be enough." – Meister Eckhart

Lord, thank you for this day. Lord, thank you for my wife and children. Lord, thank you for my family born of blood and my family built in this lifetime. Lord, thank you to all who choose to be my friend. I am honored.

Scripture of the day: 1 John 4:19
"We love because He first loved us."

Day 267: 33 RPMs

"Trust the wait. Embrace the uncertainty. Enjoy the beauty of becoming. When nothing is certain, anything is possible."
– Mandy Hale

This is the season to find your song. Records like to be played at two speeds or RPMs – 45 or 33. The RPMs, or revolutions per minute, determine how much music you would get. 45 RPMs equals one song, while 33 RPMs would allow for five or more songs. By now, we've come to an understanding that life is a long playing album played at 33 RPMs. You may not know what song is coming up next, but slow down and read the liner notes in your Bible.

Surely, you will look up one day with forced hands and say *That's my song*.

Scripture of the day: Psalm 47:1
"Oh, clap your hands, all you peoples! Shout to God with the voice of triumph!"

Day 268: Gone Girl

"She was unstoppable, not because she did not have failures of doubts, but because she continued despite of them." – Beau Taplin

It's funny, the descriptors people come up with to describe the things they don't understand. People use the terms "awesome", "incredible", "wonderful", and "amazing" – which are all very good and effective in describing the average woman, however black women have never been average.

So today, we celebrate Black Girl Magic. Yes, you are beautiful, resilient, strong, and got it going on. We could not and would not live without you.

Scripture of the day: Proverbs 31:25
"Strength and honor are her clothing; she shall rejoice in time to come."

Day 269: You Are Not Alone

"So wear your strongest posture now, and see your hardest time as more than just the times you fell, but as a mountain you learned to climb." – Morgan Harper Nichols

Take that bend out of your legs and that hunch out of your shoulders and cast your cares on the Lord. Sisyphus had his rock, Hercules fought for revenge, but Paul had his purpose and you – you know what you've been called to do. Yes, the hard times have come and there may be a few more that remain, but know that you have climbed this mountain alone before and it was difficult. This time, cast your burdens upon the Lord. He will carry you to the mountain top.

Scripture of the day: Psalm 46:1-2
"God is our refuge and strength, a very present help in trouble. Therefore, we will not fear, even though the Earth be removed, and though the mountains be carried into the midst of the sea."

Day 270: Understandable You

"I bent until I almost broke, but that's the thing about resilience – it just shows up as your soul begins to cry and catapults your strength into overdrive." – Alfa

There comes a day when you are all you can stand and can't stand any more. You feel yourself wanting to give up, but that is not you. Giving up is for the scared and you aren't the scary type.

Sure, you will bend, but breaking ain't an option for you. No, you go from strength to strength.

Scripture of the day: Hebrews 10:36
"For you have need of endurance, so that after you have done the will of God, you may receive the promise:"

Day 271: Keep Going!

"Keep Going." – Harriet Tubman

When you have decided on your goal – get on the path and keep going. When you get tired, keep going. When you doubt yourself, keep going. When the haters appear, the liars lie, and the illness falls, keep going.

No matter what, you must keep going.

Scripture of the day: Galatians 6:9
"And let us not grow weary while doing good, for in due season we shall reap if we do not lose heart."

Day 272: Use Your Gift

"Everyone is gifted but most never open their package." – Wolfgang Reibe

Most of us spend our lives afraid to rip the wrapping off these incredible gifts. We treat life and purpose as if they are gifts under the tree. You see your name on it, you will even hold it to the light and shake it, but as soon as you hear footsteps, you will stick it back under the tree, pretending it's not your gift.

Listen, you are marvelous – a creation made by God endowed with brilliance, talent, and unimaginable power. The time has arrived for you to rip the wrapping paper off your gift. Show the world how incredible you really are.

Scripture of the day: 2 Corinthians 9:15
"Thanks be to God for his indescribable gift!"

Day 273: You Are Here; Fight The Part

"One small crack does not mean that you are broken; it means that you were put to the test and you didn't fall apart."
– Linda Poindexter

You have lived through every threat and life that has come against you. You have taken every blow and rock thrown in your direction. You are banged up, chipped, battered, and a few small pieces have been broken off, yet here you still stand. All are evidence of a life that has been lived, so now you face a new foe bent on your destruction.

The funny thing is that through all the struggles, fights, and sleepless nights, you wake to face a new day. You look into the sun, not as someone who licks the wounds or pouts asking *why me* – no, you begin the day with a question for those who dare challenge your will or get in the way of your divine calling:

Who's next?

Scripture of the day: 2 Chronicles 15:7
"But you, be strong and do not let your hands be weak, for your work shall be rewarded!"

Day 274: Girl, Go Change the World

"If you are still looking for that one person that will change your life, take a look in the mirror." - Roman Price

You can search the world over and you will never find a reflection in a mirror more distinguished, true or more capable of chasing the world than your very own. You can change the world by simply walking into the room, so my sister, walk over to that mirror and repeat after me:

Hello, world changer. It's time to go make change.

Scripture of the day: Proverbs 23:18
"For surely there is a hereafter, and your hope will not be cut off."

Day 275: Rock Steady

"God's peace is not the calm after the storm. It's the steadfastness during it." – Dr. Michelle Bengston

Look at you! You have defied all expectations of your survival of that storm. You know there were a few who did not think you would make it. Truth be told, there was a couple of days you stood on the edge of the precipice with one foot all the way in.

Well, thanks be unto God who gives us the victory not over the storm, but the strength to endure, fight through, and come out on the other side stronger and all the better. Thank God for his steady hand for without Him on your side, you don't know where you would be.

Scripture of the day: Ephesians 2:8
"For by grace you have been saved through faith, and that not of yourselves; it is the gift of God,"

Day 276: The World Is Waiting

"Allow yourself to grow and change. Your future self is waiting." – Unknown

Give yourself permission to finally be free, to do, and to change. There is a strange tragedy that so many of us allow to occur in our lives. The tragedy is we force ourselves into a box of conformity. We conform to this rigid existence that does not allow for change, and I'm not talking about consistency – I'm talking about remaining the same because that's all you know.

I get it and more importantly, I understand. However, in this season, we must risk change. Start with basic change – go a different direction to work or learn a new skill. The world needs you and all that you are in order to be better.

Scripture of the day: Romans 8:21-22
"Because the creation itself also will be delivered from the bondage of corruption into the glorious liberty of the children of God. For we know that the whole creation groans and labors with birth pangs together until now."

Day 277: Walk with Power

"What matters most is how well you walk through fire." –
Charles Bukowski

One thing is for certain and two things for sure – you are in
a fight and you are going to win. Some battles in life seem
like a long, slow walk through hell, but for us, it's a walk we
will gladly take to reclaim our lives, protect those we love
and to fight for what's right.

The thing about fire is it's always hot, and it will consume
you if you stand still. Us warriors who proudly carry the
blood stained banner know all too well that we must continue
to move forward for we are on the path of righteousness.

You are trained and ready for the walk through fire,

Scripture of the day: Romans 15:13
*"Now may the God of hope fill you with all joy and peace in
believing that you may abound in hope by the power of the
Holy Spirit."*

Day 278: Risk Yourself

"The unknown future is scary, but what's scarier is not taking a leap in yourself." – Unknown

Stop worrying about tomorrow. You must boldly step into your future. There are so many wonderful things there for you – freedom, joy, and so much peace.

Come on out here and take a risk on you. You'll be amazed at how great you are.

Scripture of the day: Proverbs 23:7
"For as he thinks in his heart, so is he."

Day 279: She Is Everything

"She has the mindset of a queen and the heart of a warrior. She is everything all at once and too much for anyone who doesn't deserve her. She is you." – R.H. Sin

She walks into the room, brilliant and bold and waves her hand as if brandishing a sword. She is a warrior queen, capable of taking care of herself and all she loves. She's bad and she knows it.

Scripture of the day: Proverbs 31:26
"She opens her mouth with wisdom, and on her tongue is the law of kindness."

Day 280: You Are A Fighter

"You are a fighter. You will not give up. There will be occasions when you stumble and you will fall, but you will stand back up. It might take longer at times, but you will stand back up and keep fighting." – Unknown

There are two groups of people in your life: those who look and those who watch. They look to see how you respond under pressure and they watch to see what you will do once you get hit. Oddly enough, they have discovered that you are a fighter and that you don't give up.

No matter the battle or foe, you may stumble, but you get back up. You stayed down a couple of times, and even you didn't think you would get up, but you did.

Always remember, you are a fighter and you don't give up.

Scripture of the day: Romans 8:28
"And we know that all things work together for good to those who love God, to those who are the called according to His purpose."

Day 281: Be the Best You!

"Be thankful for what you are now, keep fighting for what you are now, and keep fighting for what you want to become tomorrow." – Unknown

It's taken a long time for you to begin to be comfortable being you. You've found yourself trying to fit into this box for her and this circle to make him happy, but neither box nor circle ever felt right because that's not what you are.

You are not a shape; you are a bold, dynamic, one-of-a-kind oxygen breathing, sweat pouring, fighting machine born to succeed and driven to seek, find, and fulfill your purpose. The New Year is drawing near, so get ready for tomorrow.

There are new battles to fight and new victories to be won, for you are on your way to becoming magnificent.

Scripture of the day: Romans 8:31
"What then shall we say to these things? If God is for us, who can be against us?"

Day 282: Are You the One?

"Out of every 100 men, ten shouldn't even be there, 80 are just targets, nine are the real fighters, and we are lucky to have them, for they make the battle. Ah, but the one, one is a warrior, and he will bring the others back." – Heraclitus

They say the darkness is coming, but you know as well as I do that it has always been dark. However, because of the sun, you are not afraid of the dark.

Our world is in need of saving. 100 will not do, the nine are fighting bravely, but only one can save them.

Are you the one?

Scripture of the day: Hebrews 7:25
"Therefore He is also able to save to the uttermost those who come to God through Him, since He always lives to make intercession for them."

Day 283: A Good Woman

"She was the type of woman who never fit in. she didn't follow the crowd or have a desire to be part of any cliques or trends, not because she wasn't good enough, but because she didn't require the approval of others. She refused to pretend to be anything she wasn't and didn't mind standing alone."
– Unknown

She moves with the confidence of someone who knows something you don't. She knows you are watching and that you dare not ask her secret. Funny as it may sound, it's no secret at all.

She knows who she is and does not care what you think. She is all that you want and everything you need all at once.

Scripture of the day: Psalm 46: 5
"God is in the midst of her, she shall not be moved;
God shall help her, just at the break of dawn."

Day 284: Stand Alone

"Always stand up for what you think is right, even if you are the only one standing." – Unknown

At some point, it becomes your turn. You will need to stand, fight, or advocate, but be not concerned with the opinions of others for why you chose to stand.

You know in your heart that standing is the right choice.

May we all be courageous and stand when our time arrives.

Scripture of the day: 1 Corinthians 16:13-14
"Watch, stand fast in the faith, be brave, be strong. Let all that you do be done with love."

Day 285: Choose Now

"Every next level of your life will demand a different you."
– Leonardo DiCaprio

You are a defender, a fighter, a leader, a survivor, and a winner. The next level is about to knock on your door. Which one of you will answer?

Scripture of the day: Ephesians 2:10
"For we are His workmanship, created in Christ Jesus for good works, which God prepared beforehand that we should walk in them."

Day 286: Self Care is the Best Care

"It's important to do what's best for you, whether people approve of it or not. This is your life. You know what's good for you and remember, self-love takes strength." – Unknown

We tend to forget that the most important person in our lives is ourselves. If there is no *you*, then there cannot be a *we*.

If you don't take care of you physically and mentally, it makes our connection that much more difficult to maintain.

Not everyone will agree that you taking care of you first is right; they may even say you are selfish, but remember this – all you have to do is die and they will soon move on. This is *your* life and self-care *is* the best care.

Scripture of the day: 3 John 1:2
"Beloved, I pray that you may prosper in all things and be in health, just as your soul prospers."

Day 287: Know Your Powers

"She is water. Powerful enough to drown you, soft enough to cleanse you and deep enough to save you." – Adrian Michael

A woman's power is like the ocean. Her power presents itself as a lot of things all at once but only the wise appreciate her vastness. She is so strong that if she gave herself to you all at once, most would drown from the overflow of her goodness. Yet her love and brilliance flow over you, washing away the stains of the past. Then just when you think she has no more to offer, you realize that you have been made stronger because of her depth, strength, love, brilliance and cleansing power.

Scripture of the day: James 1:17
"Every good gift and every perfect gift is from above, and comes down from the Father of lights, with whom there is no variation or shadow of turning."

Day 288: Act or Don't

"Complaining is silly. Either act or forget." – Stefan Sagmeister

The storm is coming and soon it will be a new year. There is no need of being afraid. No need to complain. Either act or don't. Know this; you can't go back: she doesn't love you, he doesn't want you, and they don't value you. Either act or don't. There are only a few days left in this year. Act now on your future or don't. It's up to you.

Scripture of the day: Psalm 34: 1-3
"I will bless the Lord at all times; His praise shall continually be in my mouth. My soul shall make its boast in the Lord, the humble shall hear of it and be glad. Oh magnify the Lord with me, and let us exalt His name together.

Day 289: Unstoppable

"The real difficulty is to overcome how you think about yourself." – Maya Angelou

They say that you will be okay. They say they have never seen anyone like you. They say you will never make it. It does not matter what they say. It only matters what you think. You think you are a champion. You think that you are unstoppable. The unstoppable champion is what you will become and as long as you believe, God will not let you fail.

Scripture of the day: 1 Thessalonians 5:18
"In everything give thanks; for this is the will of God in Christ Jesus for you."

Day 290: Get Up Day

"You can rise up from anything. You can completely recreate yourself. Nothing is permanent. You're not stuck. You have choices. You can think new thoughts. You can learn something new. You can create new habits. All that matters is that you decide today and never look back." – Idil Ahmed

You can be anything you want to be, however, there is only one true choice – you must be your authentic self. The old you no longer matters and woe to the man or woman who judges you by who you once were. You are no longer captured and enslaved by frivolous expectations; the time has come to think new thoughts.

Dig this – the time has come for reliable solutions and only you can solve your problems.

Scripture of the day: Deuteronomy 8:18
"And you shall remember the Lord your God, for it is He who gives you power to get wealth, that He may establish His covenant which He swore to your fathers, as it is this day."

Day 291: Begin Finished

"There will come a time when you believe everything is finished. That will be the beginning." – Louis L'Amour

The end of the year is drawing near. Use the coming days to review this past year. Use this time to cast your vision for the coming year.

Scripture of the day: 2 Corinthians 5:17
"Therefore, if anyone is in Christ, he is a new creation; old things have passed away; behold, all things have become new."

Day 292: My Friend

"A good man carries himself by how he carries his family."
– Unknown

Surely, men strive to be the best they can. They fight daily forces that align themselves against them including temptation, joblessness, mental health, love and fatherhood.

Many men have lost their lives fighting to regain their dignity, respect and protecting their integrity.

The righteous man is bolder, braver and stronger than the average man. He is a man who protects all his people. He is so powerful in his God-loving heart that his strength is only visible to those he holds near.

He is not an athlete, not a hero, but a righteous man.

Scripture of the day: 1 Corinthians 16: 13
"Watch, stand fast in the faith, be brave, be strong."

Day 293: Worth It

"Nobody can save you but yourself and you are worth saving. It's a war not easily won but if anything is worth winning this is it." – Charles Bukowski

The time has arrived. You've heard the drumbeats off in the distance for quite some time, as if some enemy was gathering its forces preparing to attack.

You stand alone now in this moment contemplating your next move, revisiting your past and pondering if it has all been worth it. You've never been alone. Your past is where it should be – behind you. Yes, you are worth it.

In the coming days there will be small skirmishes to cause you nuisance. You must remain focused. No battle is easily entered and no war is easily fought, however, this is a fight you *will* win.

This is your life.

This is your future. Thine will be done.

Scripture of the day: Proverbs 16: 3
"Commit your works to the Lord, and your thoughts will be established."

Day 294: Speak Quietly

"It's not the lion's roar that signals danger it's the silence."-Unknown

No more talking, no more words, and no more texting about every move.

Your circle is small, so whisper truth amongst yourselves. You must move in silence for the remainder of the year.

Let your completed achievements speak for you. Move with purpose, move with intention, and move with completeness. You are destined for greatness and your potential emanates from you. Stealth is your friend and silence is your calling card; let your silence speak out loud.

Scripture of the day: Job 13:5
"Oh, that you would be silent, and it would be your wisdom!"

Day 295: Fear Not

"If you're scared, just be scarier than whatever is scaring you!"- from the movie *Bambi*

You were created to fear no man.

They talk about you behind your back because they are afraid to say it to your face.

It's time for you to put fear in those who would have you be afraid.

Speak with truth, stand your ground, love who you want, and pray at all times.

By far, you are the brightest star in the soulless sky.

So, be bigger than your problems, wiser than your haters and stronger than those who would dare to stand against you.

For once let fear be afraid of you knocking on its door.

Scripture of the day: Isaiah 35:4
"Say to those who are fearful-hearted, 'be strong, do not fear! Behold, your God will come with vengeance, with the recompense of God; He will come and save you.'"

Day 296: Always Attack

"Instead of waiting to see what might develop, attack constantly, vigorously, and viciously. Never let up, never stop, always attack." – General George S. Patton

In this season you must learn to fight in a new way. You must go on the attack and attack with all your might. You must constantly be on the attack with new ideas, new solutions and with a new you. You must stay focused; you must be vicious in your intentions to vigorously surpass all you have ever done. Be relentless and no stopping.

Scripture of the day: John 15:7
"If you abide in Me, and My words abide in you, you will ask what you desire, and it shall be done for you."

Day 297: Above the Fray Always

"But I say to you, love your enemies bless those who curse you. Do good to those who hate you and pray for those who spitefully use you and persecute." – Matthew 5:44

It would so easy to do unto others as they would do unto you, but to have you do what would cause you to move further away from God is the trick of sin. So, pray for those who would do you harm, for they know not what they do, for they do not know who you are and whose you are.

Scripture of the day: 2 Peter 1:2
"Grace and peace be multiplied to you in the knowledge of God and of Jesus our Lord."

Day 298: Prove it to You!

"Be brave enough to travel the unknown path and learn what you are really capable of." – Rachel Wolchin

It is time to come from in between the rock and the hard place. The anxiety that you heap upon yourself as you move from task to task can be daunting, even for the most accomplished. Today, move onto what has been for you on an unwanted and unknown path: the path of exploration, the path of being good enough and the path of promise.

Yes, promise yourself you will show the world what you are truly capable of; you are amazing. There is no need to continue to hold back.

Scripture of the day: Hebrews 10:36
"For you have need of endurance, so that after you have done the will of God, you may receive the promise."

Day 299: More than a Woman

"She is more than a good woman and a good person. She is a beautiful soul who carries light in her smile and love in her bones." – Pierre Jeanty

To be better than most in a world that constantly compares you to everyone that has come before you is exhausting. Look at the woman you love and understand that she is more than just a good woman - she is proud, strong, and patient. Then you realize that her morality, kinship, and individuality are the things about her that turn you on. Her beauty is much deeper than her appearance; beautiful – yes, poised – yes, and a soul deep enough to love even you – yes.

Let it not be mistaken – the light that comes from her cannot easily be turned on and off. Her love is bone deep, God-given, and eternally cared for.

She is a good woman and her soul is lit by the Son.

Scripture of the day: Psalm 139: 13-14
"For You formed my inward parts; you covered me in my mother's womb. I will praise You, for I am fearfully and wonderfully made; marvelous are Your works, and that my soul knows very well."

Day 300: Patient Faith

"Be patient while this plays out. Some of you are losing your mind about something God has already worked out." – Unknown

The temptation to rush God with your miracle can be overwhelming. Who would have thought that hurrying up or waiting would require so much patience and faith?

I can only speak for myself, but there have been moments when I have been on the verge of losing my mind waiting on God's deliverance. I am learning to dial it back and stop pacing the floor searching for answers. Instead, I am choosing to believe in what I claim: that if it's for me, God has already worked it out.

Scripture of the day: 1 Timothy 4:10
"For to this end we both labor and suffer reproach, because we trust in the living God, who is the Savior of all men, especially of those who believe."

Made in the USA
Middletown, DE
18 March 2020